C. J. Thompson

Excelling at Dog Agility

Book 1: Obstacle Training

Jane Simmons-Moake

 *FlashPaws Productions*

Excelling at Dog Agility
Book 1: Obstacle Training

Illustrators: Jane Simmons-Moake, Gordon Simmons-Moake, Charles Simmons, Linda Taylor

Photographs: Jane Simmons-Moake, unless otherwise noted

Editors: Gordon Simmons-Moake, Susan Roehm, Renee Toth, Harriet Patrick, Maggie Downey, Jan Downey, Lois Williams

Cover photo: OTCh, ADCh, SKC-Ch, U-CDX Tejas Trace of Topaz, UDX, MX, AXJ, FDCh, JH, WC, VCX, OD. Photo by Jane Simmons-Moake

FlashPaws Productions
7714 Rolling Fork Lane
Houston, TX 77040-3432

Library of Congress Catalog Card Number: 99-091163

ISBN 0-9674929-0-4

Limits of Liability and Disclaimer of Warranty
The author and publisher shall not be liable in the event of incidental or consequential damages in connection with, or arising out of, the furnishing, performance, or use of the instructions and suggestions contained in this book.

First Printing, 1999

Printed in the United States of America

Contents

Dogs Appearing in this Book:

- Jack Russell Terrier *Action Jackson*, ADCh, MX, MXJ, FDX, CGC, owned by Renee Toth

- German Shorthaired Pointer *Cricket*, Ch, TDX, AD, NA, CD, Can CD, owned by Nita Chambers

- All-American *Harley*, AAD, NAC, NGC, NJC, RS-N, GS-N, JS-N, owned by Annette Dias

- Beagle *Bandit*, CDX, TDX, OA, CGC, owned by Sandy Bass

- Border Terrier *Sadie*, ADCh, CD, MX, MXJ, ME, CG, VE, CGC, owned by Jan Downey

- Golden Retriever *Kelsey*, ADCh, CD, MX, MXJ, EAC, OJC, OGC, RS-E, JS-O, GS-O, CGC, owned by Maggie Downey

- Golden Retriever *Jake*, MX, AXJ, AAD, NAC, RS-N, CGC, owned by Susan Roehm

- Border Collie *Nitro*, ADCh, FDCh, MX, CGC, owned by Lisa Layton

- Shetland Sheepdog *Ted*, ADCh, MX. MXJ, owned by Linda Barrett

- Golden Retriever *Sunny*, NA, CGC, owned by Lois Williams

- Cocker Spaniel *Sydney*, Ch, MX, MXJ, MAD, GM, OAC, OJC, OGC, RS-O, JS-O, GS-O, CGC, owned by Harriet Patrick

- Cocker Spaniel *Cody*, MX, MXJ, AAD, RM, OAC, OJC, OGC, RS-O, GS-O, owned by James and Linda Taylor

- Golden Retrievers *Holly*, ADCh, MX, MXJ, UDX, BDA-CD, and *Tracy*, OTCh, ADCh, SKC-Ch, U-CDX, UDX, MX, AXJ, FDCh, JH, WC, VCX, OD, owned by Jane Simmons-Moake

- German Shepherds *Spirit*, OTCh, UDX, ADCh, MX, FDCh, OTD-s, STD-c, STD-d, BDA-CD and *Xena*, MX, MXJ, AAD, owned by Gordon Simmons-Moake

- Border Collie *Larrie*, ADCh, MX, MXJ, CGC, owned by Gerry and Kathy Brown

- Papillon *Andy*, OA, OAJ,OAC, OJC, NGC, RS-O,JS-O, GS-N, owned by Lanelle Rachel

- Jack Russell Terrier *Polo*, OA, OAJ, AD, FM, JRTCA I and II Agility, NAC, NJC, OGC, RS-N, JS-N, GS-O, CGC, owned by Jane Tholan

- Jack Russell Terrier *Tucker*, NA, NAJ, owned by Anna Carr

Acknowledgments

Sincere thanks to the following people who helped make this book series possible:

- Renee Toth for always being there and for keeping Flash-Paws on track while I worked to finish this project.

- Gordon Simmons-Moake, Susan Roehm, Lois Williams, Renee Toth, Maggie Downey, Jan Downey, and Harriet Patrick, for their expert help in reviewing the manuscript.

- Charles Simmons, Gordon Simmons-Moake, and Linda Taylor, for their superb illustrations.

- Barbara Cecil and Gerianne Darnell, for their valuable advice on publishing.

- Wendy Volhard, for allowing me to include her Puppy Aptitude Test.

- Our wonderful students and their dogs who make it all worthwhile by providing continuous support and inspiration.

The author and Holly, ADCh, UDX, MX, MXJ, BDA-CD.

About Book 1

Welcome to *Book 1: Obstacle Training* — the first in a three-volume set entitled *Excelling at Dog Agility*. Whether you are totally new to the sport or are a seasoned veteran, *Book 1* is an excellent place to start. Within its pages you will find essential foundation principles for guiding all of your future agility training. Great emphasis is placed on training for excellence from the start, so that no retraining will be necessary later down the line. With the knowledge and skills gained from *Book 1*, you and your dog will gain a solid foundation to enable you to continue with *Book 2: Sequence Training* and *Book 3: Advanced Skills Training*.

The topics and exercises in the three books of this series correspond with three tapes of the award-winning video series entitled *Competitive Agility Training with Jane Simmons-Moake*. You may find it a helpful resource to refer to the exercises on the video tapes. Seeing the exercises demonstrated can add an extra dimension to the text and illustrations presented in this book.

You can find more information about the *Competitive Agility Training* video series at the back of this book.

Nothing is more fun than agility! (Photo: Tien Tran Photography)

_1_ The World of Competitive Agility

It seems that much of the world is now acquainted with dog agility — the rapidly growing sport in which handlers direct their dogs through challenging obstacle courses while striving for speed and accuracy. Agility is truly an international dog sport that has captured the interest of dog lovers worldwide. Spectators admire agility for its fast pace, the visually spectacular and challenging obstacles, and the contagious enthusiasm displayed by the dogs and handlers. Exhibitors love agility because it strengthens the bond between themselves and their dogs, while providing a thrilling, fast-paced competition on unique and challenging courses. As a result, newcomers to competitive agility often become hopelessly addicted — enslaved to the quest to achieve the ultimate in teamwork with their canine companion!

Watching the best agility competitors is like watching poetry in motion. No dog or handler motion is wasted. Every handler movement and command is planned and executed to communicate clearly and immediately which path the dog should take. In turn, the dog immediately interprets the handler's cues and complies with confidence, turning in a fast, exuberant, and flawless performance. Once bitten by the agility bug, this impressive level of performance becomes the goal you are forever striving to achieve.

This book is for you if you are trying to achieve a high level of dog/handler teamwork, while having a great time with your dog. It is also for you if you aren't yet sure whether you will want to compete but want to begin your training with the highest standards in mind. By following this program, if you *do* decide to compete, you will have formed only beneficial dog and handler habits. As a result, no retraining will be necessary should you choose to enter the competition ring.

Agility — An International Dog Sport

Dog agility was first introduced in 1978 by the British at the world-famous Crufts dog show. The sport was an immediate hit with both exhibitors and spectators. Not surprisingly, agility soon spread to virtually every other country on the European continent. Since then, agility has taken hold in almost every corner of the globe — including North America, Australia, New Zealand, South America, Asia, and Africa.

Agility in North America

The United States and Canada became active in the sport in the 1980's. In 1986, Kenneth Tatsch founded **the United States Dog Agility Association (USDAA),** closely following the style of agility introduced by the British. In 1990, the US-DAA began offering agility titles — certifications of accomplishment at different levels. Since then, several other North-American agility organizations have been established and have begun offering their own agility titling programs.

In 1988, Art Newman founded the **Agility Dog Association of Canada (ADAC),** dedicated to the promotion of uniform and safe standards for dog agility in Canada. This organization has grown tremendously and is now known as the **Agility Association of Canada (AAC).**

In 1993, Sharon Nelson, Jacquelyn Taylor, and Sandra Katzen formed the **North American Dog Agility Council (NADAC).** NADAC offers an enjoyable version of the sport that appeals to those who prefer its flowing course-design concept and more lenient scoring philosophy. In 1994, the **Australian Shepherd Club of America (ASCA)** adopted NADAC rules for its own agility titling program.

With such a rapidly growing number of enthusiasts becoming hooked on agility, it was only a matter of time before the **American Kennel Club (AKC)** embraced the sport. The long-awaited AKC agility titling program was launched in 1994 with a gala event inside the air-conditioned, fully sodded Astroarena, part of the huge Astrodome complex in Houston, Texas. Unlike other agility titles, AKC titles become a part of the dog's official AKC-registered name and appear on certified pedigrees, along with AKC conformation, obedience, and other working titles.

The AKC agility titling program was launched in 1994 with a gala event at the fully-sodded Houston Astroarena. (Photo: Diane Vasey)

The AKC, USDAA, AAC, and NADAC/ASCA programs differ somewhat in their equipment specifications, scoring, and titling requirements; however, all provide the excitement, course challenges, and spectator appeal found worldwide in international-style agility.

Also worth noting, a markedly different style of agility was created in 1987 by Charles "Bud" Kramer, founder of the National Club for Dog Agility (NCDA). The administration of this agility program was transferred to the **United Kennel Club (UKC)** in 1994. UKC agility is designed to be set up in small locations with limited ring space. The obstacles are smaller and are placed relatively close to one another in the competition ring. The scoring of UKC agility places emphasis on tight control throughout the course and de-emphasizes speed. To achieve the control required, and to negotiate through the obstacles in a small ring, the handlers and dogs normally work close to one another at a relatively slow, steady pace throughout the course.

In contrast, the international style of agility provides relatively large rings with much more generous spacing between obstacles. The courses provide open areas where dogs may perform at their full speed, alternating with areas requiring tighter control. The scoring emphasis is on both speed and accuracy.

Because of its differences in scoring philosophy, course size, and course layout, the skills necessary to be successful in UKC agility are different from those necessary to be competitive in international-style agility. This book focuses only on international-style agility training. It uses obstacles and course designs similar to those used internationally and by AKC, USDAA, AAC, and NADAC/ASCA.

International-Style Agility — An Overview

Obstacles

All styles of international agility share the same basic obstacles, with minor variations.

TUNNELS

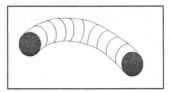

Agility courses contain two types of tunnels: **open tunnels** (sometimes called **pipe tunnels**) and **closed tunnels** (also called **collapsed tunnels**). Open tunnels are flexible tubes

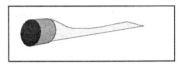

that can be arranged in a variety of curved shapes. Closed tunnels are straight and consist of a short, rigid opening followed by a long, flat, fabric chute through which the dogs must pass.

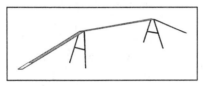

CONTACT OBSTACLES

The contact obstacles include the **dog walk, A-frame and see-saw.** All

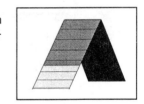

have ramps the dogs must climb and descend. The bottom portion of each ramp is painted in a contrasting color and is designated as a **contact zone** (sometimes called a **safety zone**). Dogs are faulted if they fail to touch the

contact zone with at least one part of one paw when descending the obstacle. Depending on the organization, they may also be required to touch the contact zone when ascending the obstacle.

WEAVE POLES

The **weave poles** are a series of up-right poles through which the dog must zigzag. To weave correctly, the dog must enter to the right of the first pole and continue weaving without skipping any of the poles. A dog's ability to weave with speed and accuracy is essential to competitive success in the agility ring.

JUMPS

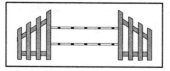

Agility courses contain a wide variety of **jumps** or **hurdles**. The style and appearance of the jumps can vary greatly from simple to wildly elaborate. Some of the jumps test the dog's ability to jump wide as well as high. These **spread jumps** may

include a broad jump or a double or triple spread jump. **Tire jumps** (jumps in which the dog jumps through the center of a tire or other circular opening) are also widely used.

PAUSE TABLE

When the course contains a pause table, the dog must jump onto the table and assume a down or sit position (as determined by the judge and/or the rules). The dog then maintains the position for a period of five seconds while the judge counts.

Course Layout and Scoring

The arrangement of the obstacles and the sequence in which they must be taken is determined by the judge. The course is never revealed ahead of time and is always different. As a result, much of the skill and strategy of agility is in preparing dogs to meet any conceivable challenge, as well as deciding which risks to take on a given course. Before competing, handlers are given a short period to "walk the course" without their dogs to memorize the course and to develop a handling strategy.

The handler must decide where to go when, and what commands to give to achieve the fastest and most accurate performance. This strategizing, in which the handler must accurately assess his dog's skills and weigh them against the possible risk of failure, is one of the most appealing facets of agility.

Most forms of agility offer a range of competitive levels. At each progressive level, courses contain more obstacles and greater challenges, such as difficult angles and frequent directional changes. Some organizations, such as the AKC, publish course design guidelines outlining the challenges that are appropriate at each level of competition. These guidelines help judges design courses that are more or less equivalent in difficulty with those of other judges. They also help the handler know what types of course challenges to expect at each level.

In competition, dogs are assessed faults for errors in obstacle performance, such as knocking down a jump bar or missing a contact zone; errors in sequencing from one obstacle to the next, such as omitting an obstacle or taking one out of sequence; and for exceeding the allotted time for a given course. Handlers may also be assessed faults for infractions such as touching their dog or touching an obstacle. At each jump height, the dog with the fewest faults wins. When there is a tie between dogs with the same number of faults, the dog with the faster time wins. Often the top placements are separated by only 10ths or even 100ths of a second.

Types of Courses

STANDARD COURSES

Standard courses are offered at virtually every agility trial, and are what most people think of when they hear the term "dog agility." In fact, many countries use the term "agility course" or "agility class" to refer to what we in the U.S. call a "standard course." These usually contain 13 - 20 obstacles which are numbered and arranged in a fixed order (Figure 1-1). Demonstrating proficiency in standard courses is necessary to earn agility titles and to participate in national tournaments.

NON-STANDARD COURSES

In addition to standard courses, many agility trials offer non-standard, or "games" classes. Certain games, such as Gamblers and Snooker, offer the handler a wide choice of options. This makes the ability to develop a unique and competitive handling strategy an important factor in determining your success in the ring.

The most common games tend to be those that are part of the requirements to earn agility titles. Several national organizations award titles that require demonstrated proficiency in one or more of the games classes. Some of the most common games include:

Jumpers: A numbered course consisting only of jumps, tunnels, and sometimes weave poles (Figure 1-2).

Gamblers: Consists of a point accumulation period followed by a very brief period in which the handler must direct his dog to perform a specified series of obstacles at a considerable distance from the handler (Figure 1-3).

Snooker: A complicated game in which strategy may dictate a contorted obstacle sequence, usually requiring a great deal of control.

Pairs Relay: Two dog/handler teams compete together as a pair. The course is configured like a standard course without a pause table. Each team runs half the course. The active handler carries a baton, which must be exchanged while all dogs and handlers are within a designated exchange area.

Knockout: All dog/handler teams are divided into pairs for direct-elimination competition. The two teams in each pair compete simultaneously and head-to-head on two short, identical courses. The winner advances to the next round.

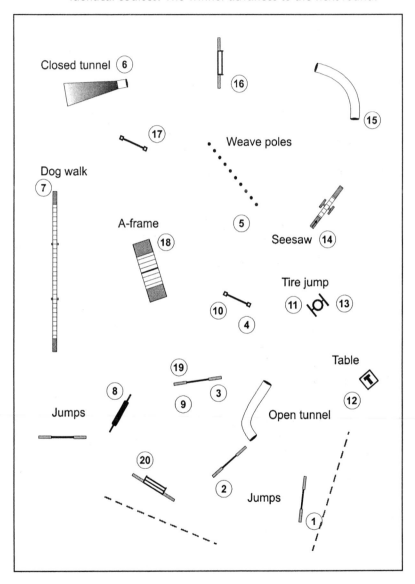

Figure 1-1: Standard course example.

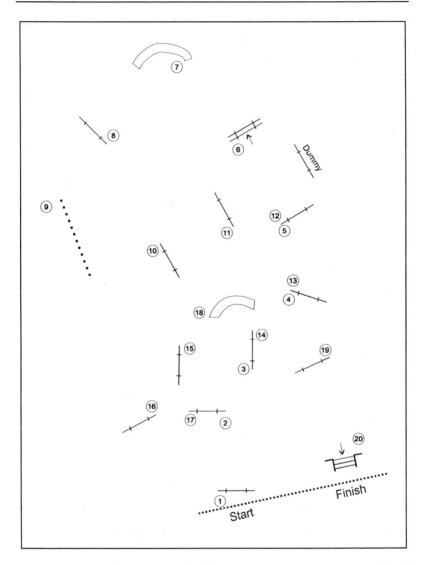

Figure 1-2: Jumpers course example. Jumpers courses consist entirely of jumps, tunnels, and sometimes weave poles.

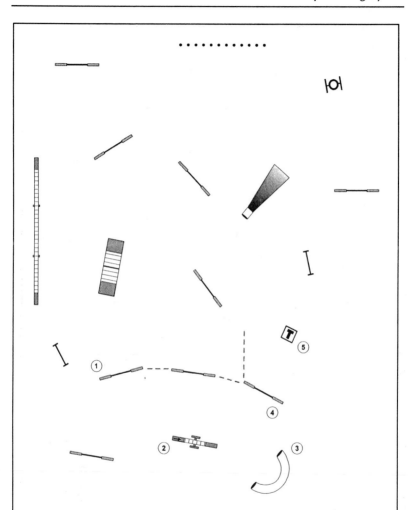

Figure 1-3: Gamblers course example. For the gamble, the handler must send the dog quickly and accurately through the obstacles marked #1 through #5 — without crossing the far side of the dotted line.

Trends in International Agility

Most countries that participate in agility now hold annual National Championship events. These events bring together the best competitors from each country to compete for top honors in each jump height division.

Beyond the honor of becoming a National Champion is the honor of becoming a World Champion. In 1996, 23 countries sent their top agility teams to Morges, Switzerland to compete in the very first **Agility World Championship** event, sponsored by the Federation Cynologique Internationale (FCI). This truly international Olympic-caliber event included teams from many European countries, as well as from Japan, Russia, and the United States.

Until fairly recently, agility exhibitors from one country knew very little about agility in other nations. The FCI Agility World Championship has helped change this situation. So has the increasing popularity of the Internet. Today, competitors worldwide share information daily via computer on a variety of agility topics. At Internet agility sites and via E-mail, agility handlers eagerly swap training tips, rumors and gossip, war stories, course diagrams, cries and brags, and handling strategies.

Once a very fragmented group, the global agility community has become a more closely knit entity, sharing their ideas and enthusiasm at an international level.

The first Agility World Championship was held in Morges Switzerland in 1996.

The United States Agility team displays their colors at the first Agility World Championship. (Left to right:) Karen Moureaux and Border Collie "Dallas," Pati Hatfield and Belgian Malinois "Lilly," Jane Simmons-Moake and Golden Retriever "Holly," Stuart Mah and Border Collie "Recce," Nancy Gyes and Border Collie "Scud," Team Captain: AKC Agility Director Sharon Anderson, AKC Vice President of Performance Events Robert McKowen.

Border collies are particularly well-suited to the sport of agility. However, they are not the right breed for everyone. (Photo: Skipper Productions)

2 Selecting Your Canine Teammate

If you already have the dog or dogs you would like to work with and are not looking for another, you may want to skip this chapter for the time being. This chapter is for those who are looking for a first or an additional dog with which to compete and excel in agility.

Considering the number of years you and your next agility prospect will be spending together, it makes sense to find one that meets your goals, personality, and lifestyle. This is not to say a perfect training companion couldn't walk up to your front door looking for a home. Realistically, however, most great things don't happen by accident.

Personality Traits

Once you become hooked on agility, you will probably develop the urge to train and compete with more than one dog. With each additional dog you train, you learn more about which qualities you want in your next dog as well as qualities you would like to avoid or minimize. When acquiring a dog with competition in mind, it pays to spend some time defining what you consider your ideal agility training partner.

Do you prefer a dog that is independent, clingy, or middle of the road? Tough, submissive, or somewhere in between? Hyperactive? Calm? Focused? Stubborn? Affectionate? Reserved? Mild-mannered? Pushy? Polite? Willing? Intelligent? Different trainers have very contrasting ideas about the ideal type of dog to train. For example, some people don't enjoy working with a dog that is constantly pushing the limits to see what it can get away with. On the other hand, some people greatly respect and admire these types of dogs, and prefer to work with them rather than those that are more passive and agreeable.

As you create your profile of the perfect agility partner, keep in mind that your description should also be compatible with the qualities you seek in a household companion. For example, wanting the fastest, most driven dog you can find may not be compatible with wanting a dog that will lie quietly at your feet for hours.

Some personality traits are undesirable in any working dog or household companion, i.e., shyness, sound sensitivity, tactile sensitivity, and fear of the unfamiliar. Socialization and training may help these dogs overcome some of their sensitivities. More often than not, however, these traits have been inherited and have little chance of being completely overcome.

Success in agility is a product of both dog and handler. The best trainer or handler in the world can only get so much out of a limited-potential dog. Undesirable characteristics such as spookiness, tactile sensitivity, advancing age, and lack of drive all limit a dog's potential. However, an excellent trainer with a limited-potential dog can often outscore a dog with excellent potential that is poorly handled and trained.

How do you assess a dog's temperament? There is no foolproof way short of living with the dog and training him for a length of time. By that time, you may have become very attached and will not want to part with your canine friend, regardless of his personality. To prevent this from happening, there are some things you can do to assess the dog's personality before you commit to making him a permanent member of your family.

You and your dog will be training partners and extremely close companions for many years to come. It makes sense to take a considerable amount of time and effort to find the perfect dog for you.

Puppy Testing

Although many people are successful at acquiring and training an older dog, you will have the best chance to mold your future agility champion if you acquire him as a puppy. When selecting a puppy from a litter, puppy aptitude testing may help you make your decision. Though far from foolproof, properly performed tests can give you a very good idea of the relative merits of each of the puppies in a litter. Among other characteristics, puppy testing can offer you some comparative information about degree of dominance or submission, social attraction, pain sensitivity, noise sensitivity, stability, energy level, and work attitude.

Although there are several standard tests from which to choose, the *Puppy Aptitude Test* developed by Wendy Volhard is one of the most popular. Besides its widespread use by breeders to match puppies with prospective owners, the *Puppy Aptitude Test* is also often used by law enforcement agencies and service organizations to select high-potential working dogs.

The best results are obtained when puppies are tested at 49 days of age. The tests should be performed by a stranger to the puppies in unfamiliar surroundings and at a time when the puppies are hungry and active. Avoid testing on a day in which the puppies have been exposed to stressful situations such as inoculations or a trip to the veterinarian. You can find a description of the Volhard *Puppy Aptitude Test* in *Appendix A.*

The Breeder as Resource

In addition to puppy testing, the breeder of the litter can often be extremely helpful in selecting the right pup. Most reputable breeders spend countless hours observing the puppies, and are likely to have made some assessments about their relative personality traits. Of particular value is advice from breeders who train and show their own dogs for performance events. They are most likely to understand and identify the characteristics desirable in a working dog.

Breeders who do not show in performance events are sometimes less apt to truly understand what you need. For example, some may equate the least attractive or least structurally sound as the agility or obedience pick. Working dogs need good structure too! Some may identify the most active puppy as the agility pick, regardless of the pup's other characteristics. The most active puppy in the litter might be perfect for your needs, or it might not. It could be a very dominant dog, or one with a lack of focus or work ethic. In a case like this, you might be more successful and enjoy the match more if you were to select a slightly less active puppy.

Selecting an Adult Dog

Not everyone wants to start with a puppy. Some prefer to skip the puppy phase and start with an adult from a shelter or a breed rescue organization. One of the advantages of doing this is that you will know pretty much what size your dog will reach. The dog may also be old enough to screen for genetic health problems such as hip dysplasia. With a puppy, you may put in several years of training only to discover that the dog has a physical problem and cannot be trained any longer. Another advantage of adopting an older dog is that you are giving a loving home to a dog that desperately needs one.

A possible disadvantage is that your rescue dog may have temperament problems that are difficult or impossible to overcome. Some formerly abused, neglected, or unsocialized dogs may never trust humans completely. They may have developed fears of people, places, sounds, or materials that can make training and showing extremely difficult. You will most likely be able to help this kind of dog overcome some of his fears through patient, gentle training and desensitization sessions. It is unlikely, however, that you will be able to overcome all of his problems.

Not all rescue dogs, however, come from backgrounds of abuse or neglect. Many are given up to shelters merely because they are high-energy animals, with owners who have neither the knowledge nor the patience to train them. With the right trainer, these can often become highly competitive agility dogs. Be prepared, however, to put in some extra work to train good habits and behaviors to replace those that resulted in his being banished to the pound.

When choosing an adult dog as an agility prospect, look for a healthy, bright-eyed, happy, and confident dog with good structure. Avoid dogs displaying fear, or excessive sensitivities to sound or touch.

Physical Attributes

Good vision, a healthy heart, and sound structure are essential if your dog is to withstand the repeated jumping, climbing, and running that agility requires.

Genetic Defects

Many serious physical problems such as cataracts, heart disorders, and hip dysplasia can be genetically transmitted and are more common than you might think. Unfortunately, many such problems are difficult or impossible to detect in puppies or young dogs. The best you can do to help ensure your agility prospect is sound is to make sure that his parents, siblings, aunts, uncles, and grandparents have been screened and are free from any serious genetic defects commonly found in the breed. This will not guarantee that your dog will not develop problems, but it will lessen the chances of a defect developing later in life.

Sound Structure

A sound dog will be able to withstand the high physical demands of agility training and competition without breaking down or sustaining an injury. A dog with one or more physical problems is likely to be a candidate for limited participation and/or early retirement from strenuous dog sports.

To help ensure a long and healthy agility career, look for a dog that has these characteristics:

- Well-angulated and balanced in front and rear

- Good rib spring for adequate lung capacity

- Adequate length of leg and neck for ease in jumping

- Compact, rounded feet with thick pads, and strong pasterns (wrists) for absorbing the impact of repeated landing

Also keep in mind that a lighter-boned, leggier dog is often likely to be faster and more agile. He may also possess greater stamina than a stockier candidate of the same breed, all other factors being equal.

Starting with an Older Dog

If your goal is to have a good time with your dog, and your dog is sound and healthy, there is nothing to prevent you from starting with a dog that is already 4 - 6 years of age. Most people find that agility training strengthens the bond between dog and owner, while opening up new worlds for both of them. Owners of all dogs who have started in agility — even those who begin later in life — report a wide variety of benefits. Some find their dogs are less timid and more confident in new situations, behave better around the house, are more comfortable around other dogs and people, and can accompany their owners to a world of new places.

Starting with an older dog is a great way to "get your feet wet" in the sport. Older dogs are generally calmer and more focused than younger dogs. They may also be slower, and therefore easier to manage for a beginning handler. Many people who start with an older dog find themselves addicted to the sport and, within a year or so, acquire a puppy or younger dog with agility competition in mind.

If your goal is to embark on an extended career in competitive agility training, consider the longevity of your breed and realistically estimate the number of years you will be able to train together. Many large dogs start to slow down at 6 to 7 years of age, sooner than most small dogs. Although most large dogs are retired from agility by 8 years of age, it's not unusual to see a small dog still competing at the age of 8 or 9.

Consider the length of time it takes to become ready to compete. Most dogs with basic obedience training can be trained to compete at the Novice level with only a few months to a year of agility training. Attaining a Novice-level title with an older dog is a very realistic goal for even an inexperienced Novice handler. To earn a higher-level title, the dog must be trained to a significantly higher standard. If you have the time, motivation, and instructional know-how, these more advanced titles are also attainable. It can take anywhere from 1 - 3 years to train your dog to be competitive at these advanced levels.

Physical Condition of the Older Dog

Ideally, the dog should be lean and muscular, with good vision, and a healthy heart. What's more, he should be free of arthritis, hip, knee, or shoulder problems, or any other debilitating condition.

Many of the dogs that come to us for beginning agility training, regardless of whether they are young or old, are carrying too many excess pounds for a working agility dog. Too much weight is undesirable in a dog of any age, but it is a particularly serious problem with an older dog. Extra weight limits the dog's stamina and places extra stress on the joints, which is exacerbated while running, climbing, and jumping. If a dog is at a good working weight, you should be able to feel his ribs easily, without feeling excess padding.

Some dogs may be sufficiently lean but may still be out of condition. Like people, older dogs that launch into a strenuous exercise program from the life of a couch potato are more prone toward muscle strains and injuries. Taking the time to develop a base level of conditioning in the older dog before beginning agility training can be very beneficial. Not only will it help to prevent injury to the dog, but the dog is more likely to have a better attitude and stamina, since he is already accustomed to a program of regular exercise.

Breed Considerations

You may already know which breed you would like to train. The breed could be one you have always owned, or one you've never owned but have come to admire. Before making a final decision on a breed, consult your list of character traits and research your chosen breed to see if the two are compatible. Although there is a wide range of personality types within any given breed, there are usually characteristics that predominate. If you know other owners of the breed, talk to them about their dogs. You can also contact a local or national breed club devoted to the breed you are considering. Such clubs can usually provide information on the breed's positive and negative characteristics, although you may have to probe for the negative ones.

It's been said that dog breeds that were originally developed to work with people (dogs from the herding, sporting, and working groups) are more likely to be willing workers than breeds that were created to work independently from people or those that were developed to be primarily companions and not working dogs. This is true on a general level; however, many highly skilled, top competition dogs come from the terrier, toy, hound, and non-sporting groups — not to mention mixed breeds. Attend an agility trial and you will see outstanding performances by breeds such as Papillons, Jack Russell Terriers, Beagles, Keeshonds, and Poodles of all sizes.

While there are wonderful agility prospects in most breeds, they are harder to find in some breeds than others. Within every breed there will be a wide range of types. This is even more pronounced within the most popular breeds, where breeders create litters to fulfill a specific purpose, such as to win in the conformation ring or to excel in field trials. As a result of this selective breeding, dogs of these popular breeds that were not specifically bred for working may have less drive, willingness to work (work ethic), and heavier-boned bodies than those bred for working.

When selecting a breed, beware of the "I-want-a-dog-just-like-so-and-so (insert impressive agility dog here) syndrome"— especially if you are new to training dogs. Find out what was necessary to train the dog you admire to achieve that level of performance. It may have taken a huge investment in training time, private lessons, strength of will, consistency, patience, creativity, energy level, and ingenuity to create the dog you see today. Often the highest potential dogs are the most difficult to train, and may be frustrating or difficult to live with.

Some people have tremendous success with dogs of breeds reputed to be difficult to train. Often their success is a result of careful selection, coupled with early training and knowing exactly what to do to groom that type of dog to be a willing worker with focused attention from day one. If you are relatively new to the world of dogs, be sure to talk to the people who have trained these wonderful dogs and ask for advice. They know better than anyone what it took to get there and can give you an idea of what is in store if you choose a similar path.

3 Training for Excellence

Do not skip this chapter! Of all the chapters in this book, it is likely to have the greatest impact on achieving your agility goals. The chapter explains important principles for training a competitive agility dog. Although some of these ideas will be repeated throughout this book, the most important concepts are presented here for you to consider before beginning your training.

Later, if your training seems to be experiencing setbacks, consider re-reading this chapter. It may serve as a reminder of important principles you already know, but may have let slide.

Set Your Standards High

A prerequisite to achieving excellence is being able to picture it in your mind. Doesn't it make sense that you need to know what you are striving for to know if you have achieved it? Agility, like peanut butter, comes in two varieties: smooth and crunchy.

If you have been a spectator at many agility trials you've probably seen plenty of crunchy agility. These are the performances that seem to be on the verge of disaster at every turn. The dog is crudely slammed and jammed into the prescribed obstacle path. Often, the dog does not realize which obstacle the handler wants him to take until the last possible moment.

Crunchy agility runs often include spins and "head checks" in which the dog turns back to the handler, seeking direction. They may also include bumping, in which the dog and handler collide while negotiating the course. These negative behaviors may be due to the handler's mistimed commands or ambiguous body language. They may also be due to skill deficiencies on the part of the dog. Head checks, bumping, and spins all contribute to lost time on the course — not to mention the increased possibility of knocked bars, runouts (the dog running past the correct obstacle), and refusals.

During crunchy agility runs, the handler often runs closely alongside the dog, sometimes interfering with his jumping style. Rather than perform side-switches to initiate smooth changes of direction, the handler may try to outrun the dog and shove him into the next obstacle. Sometimes this is successful, sometimes it is not. From the stands, the spectator is on the edge of his seat, wondering if the dog and handler will be able to make it through the course without faulting.

Contrast this with smooth agility, where timely commands and consistent body cues are delivered from a comfortable distance, so as not to interfere with the dog's movement. The dog's head never turns back on his fast-moving, forward path and his jumping style is smooth and fluid. To the observer in the stands, the handler and dog appear to be in perfect sync, working together, yet separately. Though the dog may be traveling at breakneck speed, the performance never appears to be on the verge of disaster. The dog's course time is further optimized because no time is wasted by spinning, checkbacks, jagged paths, or by the dog hanging back to keep pace with his handler. Although some people prefer to train and handle in a "crunchy" manner, this book is intended to help those who aspire to the "smooth agility" picture of perfection.

Knowing which behaviors you want to develop is as important as knowing which behaviors you don't want from your future agility star. Some unwanted behaviors include:

- Refusals/runouts

- Head checks

- Spinning

- Barking

- Sniffing

- Attention lapses

- Lack of enthusiasm

- Lack of speed

- Lack of accuracy of obstacle performance

- Delayed responses to commands

During your training sessions, if you observe any of these behaviors, stop right away and fix them! Think about how you can get the dog to perform the skill to more closely match your standards. It may require additional motivation or training aids, but you should be able to devise a way to get the behavior you want. Repeating poor behavior (or, worse yet, rewarding it) is only likely to strengthen the unwanted behavior, making it more difficult to retrain when you finally decide you've had enough of it. What's more, by ignoring the problem and continuing, you have lost an opportunity to isolate the deficient skill and shape it in a direction that more closely matches your mental picture of perfection.

Our dogs are only as skilled as we ask them to be. Train yourself to notice even the slightest deviation from perfection and work to improve it. You need never settle for mediocrity!

Concentrate on Skill-Building

Once a dog has mastered the individual obstacles, many trainers are eager to start running long sequences or entire courses as soon as possible. Running courses is an important and necessary part of training for both handler and dog, but it is secondary in importance to developing the skills — both handler skills and dog skills — that you will need to complete agility courses smoothly. Resist the urge to set up entire courses just to be "doing agility." Although you and your dog may both have a good time, in most cases you are teaching your dog very little. What's more, if you ignore mistakes in an effort to complete the course uninterrupted or to "get a time," you have reinforced your dog for performing incorrectly. As a result, your dog is more likely to repeat mistakes at a later date — in the competition ring!

To make the most out of your training time, the largest part of your training should be skill development — teaching or strengthening skills you and your dog will need to excel in competition. Most skills can be trained using only one to three obstacles. When training new skills, train only one skill per exercise. Later, when the skills become stronger, you can combine several skills in one exercise. Just remember to stop immediately when a problem occurs.

Develop a Plan

It is a good practice to have everything ready for your training session before bringing your dog to the training area. Pre-planning will minimize downtime between exercises. At the same time, it will keep your dog focused on you and enjoying his work. Too much downtime can result in your dog becoming bored or engaging in other activities. Your pre-training preparation should include the following:

- List the skills on which you want to work.

- Devise exercises to work on these skills.

- Collect all the training equipment and supplies you will need to carry out your plan.

- Set up your equipment in the planned configurations.

If, despite following your plan, your dog goes exploring or chasing squirrels between exercises, you are probably not making your training sessions interesting enough. Alternatively, you may not be moving briskly enough from one exercise to the next. Your training sessions should be the highlight of your dog's day! Keeping your sessions short makes it easier to keep your training moving, with your dog fully engaged from one exercise to the next.

After each session, make notes about your goals for future sessions. This is particularly important if you train more than one dog at a time. Include comments about what worked, what didn't work, and any new deficiencies you noticed. When shaping a new skill, be sure to note the progress you've made so that you can build on that skill during the next training session.

Avoid Training Alone

Even the most accomplished agility trainers are better off if they train with a partner or with an instructor. Training alone makes it too easy to let mistakes slide, or — worse yet — become reinforced! Working with someone else helps keep you "honest" in your training. When you work alone, you may be more likely to blame the dog for a mistake that is actually your own. A partner or instructor can help provide important feedback about whether your commands are on time, and whether your signals and body movements are clear and consistent from the dog's point of view. Good trainers always appreciate friendly nagging. They know it can play a significant role in refining their dog/handler teamwork.

Less is More — Don't Over-Train

Speed is as essential element in becoming competitive in agility, and in remaining competitive throughout your dog's agility career. Though a dog's speed can be affected by environmental elements such as the weather, speed is primarily a result of the dog's drive and enthusiasm for the sport. This enthusiasm also plays a large role in how hard he tries to work with you and comply with your rules of the game. To maintain enthusiasm, agility training should be a special treat available to the dog in short, intense sessions, rather than in long, unenthusiastic marathons with extensive, repetitive drilling.

Every dog is different. Some can withstand longer sessions and can endure more repetitions than others. Keep alert for signs that your dog is becoming tired or bored. The key to maintaining attitude is to end your sessions with the dog wanting more. If you are doing your job, the dog should be disappointed that the session is over — he should definitely not be relieved! To this end, don't end your sessions with a fun game of ball or by letting the dogs chase each other around the field. They might spend the entire session looking forward to the moment when it is over. Instead, intersperse games and play throughout your training sessions at unpredictable intervals.

If your dog tires easily, check his weight. You should be able to feel his ribs without much effort. Giving your dog regular exercise outside of your agility training will help keep him lean and well-muscled for jumping and climbing. What's more, a dog in lean, muscular condition will have greater stamina and will be less prone to injuries.

Always quit while your dog still wants to do more.

Control Your Tone of Voice

In all of your training, be aware of your tone of voice. Work with a partner or tape record a training session or two. Your voice commands should be pleasant, clear, confident, and enthusiastic. Your tone should be interesting, not monotone. All praise should sound sincere, not robot-like or gratuitous. Dogs tend to tune out handlers who use a relentlessly high-pitched, chirpy (or begging) tone of voice. Likewise, you are bound to lose attitude if you bellow your commands like an army sergeant. You might even be penalized for it later in the agility ring. Enunciate your commands clearly — don't mumble! The more confident you sound, the more your dog will have confidence in you as a team leader.

If you have a dog that is either extremely excitable or very easy-going, you may benefit from adjusting your tone of voice to suit your dog's temperament. The more excitable or frantic your dog is, the calmer and more controlled your voice will need to be. Conversely, to get the most out of a slower, more tentative dog, you will need to inject a generous amount of enthusiasm and excitement in your commands and praise.

Begin Your Training as Early as Possible

Whether starting with an older dog or a puppy, teach your new agility partner to love to work and learn with you from the moment he enters your household. Although it is possible to achieve remarkable success when starting agility with an older dog, the road may be smoother and you may realize greater potential if you start with a young puppy. Seven weeks of age is ideal. Older dogs may come to you with existing behavior or temperament problems. They may also have developed poor attitudes toward working with people, which may be difficult to completely overcome.

A seven-week old puppy's mind is a blank slate, ready to be programmed for success. When he leaves his littermates and comes to live with you, your pup has no idea of what life has in store for him. You now have a wonderful opportunity to show him that life is about learning and working with people, and that working together is fun and rewarding.

People who prefer that their dog "be a puppy for a year" before starting any training are missing out on the most influential learning and imprinting period in their dog's lifetime. What's more, when giving a puppy this important first year off, the puppy learns few rules, develops no work ethic or joy of learning, and has little reason to please anyone but himself. When training eventually begins, the party is literally over, and the dog may be reluctant or even resentful when asked to work for things that he once received for free.

Early training and development of a good attitude toward work is especially important with breeds that were not primarily intended for working with people. If you have selected one of these more challenging breeds, don't miss this critical period in your puppy's life to let him know he is destined to become a working dog.

To develop a good attitude toward learning, your early training should be entirely positive and motivational. Teaching your puppy some cute party tricks such as beg, wave, or roll-over, is a great way to get your puppy to love learning and working with you. Be sure to also include important obedience commands such as sit, down, and come. Many agility skills can also be learned at a very early age, all at very low, safe heights. As a result, your pup can gain many of the advanced-level skills necessary to compete, before he is even old enough to begin jumping his full competition height.

Sending to the tunnel from various angles and distances is a fun and safe training activity for puppies.

Use a Varied and Unpredictable Reward Schedule

To teach and strengthen desirable behaviors, it helps to use a variety of reinforcers, or rewards. A reward is anything your dog likes. Common training rewards include food treats, balls, toys, pats on the chest or head, or silly games with the handler. The more things you can find that your dog likes, the more buttons you will have available to push should your dog's interest begin to wane. Using a variety of reinforcers makes the training session much more interesting for the dog since he never knows what reward he's trading his behavior for — a tossed ball, a kernel of kibble, or a big chunk of fresh liver.

All of us tend to settle into ruts. We end up doling out a one-centimeter-sized slice of hot-dog (or whatever your usual bait might be) for each reward. We even get into the habit of rewarding on a fixed ratio or schedule, such as every third correct response or approximately every two minutes. You can get more out of your dog if you work hard to avoid falling into these predictable patterns of reinforcement.

To keep your dog working with enthusiasm, vary the type, quantity, and interval of your rewards. If training with food, fill your pocket with a mixture of treats ranging from delectable to ho-hum. If he never knows what, when, or how much of a reward he will receive, he will be more attentive and will work harder to hit a jackpot.

The same approach works for dogs that are toy-motivated. To keep your dog enthusiastic, hide a variety of toys inside your clothes or training bag and produce one or more of them as a reward at an unexpected moment.

It helps to have many types of rewards of varying strengths available so that the dog never knows what reward to expect for the correct behavior. If you have a dog with a limited number of buttons to push, it's never too late to develop additional reinforcers. For example, for a dog that goes wild for liver but little else, you could try making a toy or a pat on the head or even a silly sound a more powerful reinforcer — something the dog will work hard to receive. To accomplish this, immediately follow the new reward you want to develop with a strong, existing reinforcer. For example, when your dog offers a correct behavior, pat him on the head, and then immediately give him a chunk of liver. Eventually, the pat on the head will elicit much more interest than it did in the past.

Welcome Your Dog's Mistakes

Mistakes are a necessary part of learning. Be happy when your dog makes them in your training sessions! How else can he learn when an option is correct and when it is not? Mistakes are golden training opportunities to communicate to your dog what you like and what you do not like. Good trainers want their dogs to make mistakes in training. Mistakes provide an opportunity to work through the problems and make them less likely to occur during competition.

When a mistake occurs, *blame the dog last.* Often the handler is responsible, due to a late or inconsistent command or an ambiguous body posture. Be happy if you discover that it is *you* that is at fault. Identifying the problem is the first step in solving it, and it is much easier to communicate what needs to be done differently to yourself than it would be to explain it to your dog.

Sometimes your dog will be at fault. Honest mistakes occur frequently in the learning stages of training any skill. When they do, give a non-emotional (or flat) verbal correction such as *Wrong!, Uh-oh!,* or *Oops!* at the precise moment of the infraction (e.g., as the dog knocks a jump bar or misses a weave pole). This communicates what was incorrect about his performance. The verbal correction is intended to be informational, not punitive. If you give a harsh correction (either verbal or physical) for an honest mistake when the dog is learning something new, he may be reluctant to try at all the next time. After your verbal correction, immediately repeat the exercise, giving extra help to make sure the dog is successful on the next try. Give extra rewards for getting it right after a mistake.

Once the dog has thoroughly learned a skill, he may still make an error. First rule out the possibility that it was caused by your handling, by the dog being fearful, or as a result of confusion. Once these are ruled out, it is likely the dog was distracted or felt he had a choice about whether or not to comply. These instances often call for a swift, non-emotional physical correction. The corrections you use, however, should only be as strong as is necessary to effect a change in behavior. Keep an upbeat attitude when giving a correction, and follow immediately with praise and an opportunity to try again.

If you are doing your job right as a trainer, you will probably need to give very few physical corrections during your agility training. If the dog's mistakes are due to weak responses to obedience commands such as *Come!* or *Stay!*, work on these problems away from the time and the place you train agility. You may then give whatever corrections may be necessary without risking damage to your dog's attitude toward agility.

_4_ Obstacle Training Principles

This chapter precedes step-by-step procedures for training each of the competition agility obstacles. There are no prerequisites for starting your obstacle training since all beginning work is on-lead.

Our principle of doing it right from the start certainly applies to obstacle training. Although it is arguably the simplest part of your agility training program, obstacle training is the critical foundation on which all your subsequent training builds. For many dogs, this will be the first time they have been asked to work with their owners. How you define your working relationship and what you expect from your dog will shape the way your dog relates to you for his entire agility career.

Setting your standards high from the start will prevent you from having to retrain later. Retraining not only takes extra time, but it seems that retrained dogs are never quite as solid and reliable as those who learned it right from the start. To keep your training on track, it helps to have established a mental picture of perfect performance for each of the obstacles. If you don't know what you are striving for, how will you know when you have achieved it?

In the chapters that follow, the training procedures for each obstacle are preceded by a sample description of a mental picture of perfect performance. Keep in mind that descriptions of perfection differ with each person and dog. However, you can use them as a starting point for you to create your own descriptions.

Principles

During your obstacle training, keep the following principles in mind. They apply to the training of all obstacles.

One Command per Obstacle

If you have spent any time as a spectator at agility events, you are sure to have watched handlers who incessantly repeat commands to their dogs. For example, a handler who repeatedly chants *"Tunnel!, Tunnel!, Tunnel!, Tunnel!"* when he wants the dog to find the tunnel and run through it.

If you get in the habit of issuing multiple commands, you run the risk of teaching your dog to tune you out — not to mention, the possibility of interfering with your ability to issue a timely command for the next obstacle. With multiple commands, the dog can easily begin to think that the way agility works is "If I don't pay attention to the first command, it's OK because Mom is bound to say it again." If your dog is traveling at a decent speed, responding to your second or third command is not an option. Your dog must respond immediately to your first command, or it becomes too late for him to comply. He can easily bypass the next obstacle or pass the point at which he can perform it without incurring a fault. Issuing repeated commands relieves the dog of the obligation of paying attention to you and becomes, in essence, begging on your part. (Please, please, pleeeeeeeease — do the tunnel!)

It makes sense that the smoothest agility runs are those in which the dog and handler each take responsibility for their own tasks. As a handler, your responsibility is to give unambiguous commands (that you have thoroughly trained your dog to understand) on time and in a clear and consistent manner. Your dog's obligation is to listen and respond promptly to your commands the first (and only) time they are given. With this system, your relationship becomes one of mutual trust and true teamwork, and your handling appears very "clean" in the ring. If you never accept anything less, this is what you will always have, and your ring performances will always speak well of your dog-handler relationship.

Choose a Different Command for Each Obstacle that Looks Different to the Dog

It can be a great advantage to have your dog recognize the obstacles by the commands you have chosen for them. When running a course, you will not always be in a position to use body language to communicate the correct obstacle. When your dog is ahead of you and running at high speed, his obstacle discrimination skills can save the day. For this reason, it is a good idea to choose a different command for each obstacle that appears different to the dog. For example, dogs can easily distinguish the tire from the tunnel by their distinct shapes; therefore, you should choose separate commands for each of these obstacles. Although some handlers choose a different command for the broad jump because of it's unique appearance, it is best to use only one command for all of the other jumps, regardless of their appearance or style.

Because your dog must process your commands in an instant at high speeds, short, distinct commands are better than longer ones. Use no more than two syllables or your speedy dog will have taken several obstacles by the time you have finished your previous command!

Make sure the commands you choose do not sound like other commands you use for agility or any other purpose. If this is your first agility competition dog, you are fortunate. Now is the time to use all knowledge available to you to make the most informed decision about choosing your commands. For years many agility old-timers used the command *Tunnel!* for the open tunnel and *Table!* for the pause table, only to discover that those words can be hard to distinguish for many dogs — especially during the excitement of competition. If you are training your first dog in agility, it would be wise to choose a different command for the pause table if you plan to use *Tunnel!* for the open tunnel.

You may wish to choose from the following list of commonly used commands. The commands in bold face form a good set that will work for most dogs.

Obstacle	Commands
Open Tunnel	*Tunnel, Through*
Closed Tunnel	*Chute, Tunnel*
Tire Jump	*Tire, Hoop, Ring*
Jumps	*Over, Hup, Jump*
Weave Poles	*Weave, Poles*
Dog Walk	*Dog Walk, Plank, Walk It, Ramp*
A-Frame	*Scramble, A-Frame, Climb, Wall*
See-Saw	*See-Saw, Teeter*
Pause Table	*Bench, Table, Rest, Pause*

Some commonly used commands for the agility obstacles.

If you are one of the old timers, you will have to decide for yourself whether it is worth it to change your commands. It can be difficult to remember a different set of commands for several dogs that you are training and showing concurrently. One possibility is to retrain your existing dogs to respond to the new commands. Then, the difficult part will be training you, the handler, not to revert to your old commands while under the stress and excitement of competition.

Work Obstacles from Both Sides from Day One

To be competitive, your dog must be able to work off both your left and your right. If you work all obstacles (including the weave poles) equally off both sides from the start, your dog will know of no other way to do agility. As a result, you will enjoy the flexibility and freedom of handling off either side in all of your training and in the ring from the day you begin competing.

People who wait until later in their training to start working with their dogs on their right sides (working *off the right*) are limited in their handling choices in early competition. (Some refer to this as working *off-side*, as if the practice were a lesser alternative to handling off the left —which it definitely is not!) Later, when the courses become too difficult to be handled entirely off the left, they face the need to retrain their dogs to work off the right. Even after a lengthy retraining effort, your dog may be somewhat less comfortable working off your right than he is off your left.

Start Sending and Calling to Obstacles ASAP

Once the dog is performing an obstacle reliably, quickly, and accurately, work on being able to send the dog to the obstacle from a distance. Your goal is to be able to send your dog to the obstacle with one command and signal from a distance of up to 30 feet and from a variety of angles. You should also be able to call your dog to each obstacle from the same angles and distances. These distance skills will provide an essential foundation for smooth sequencing work.

In all of your obstacle training, start sending your dog to the obstacles as soon as possible.

Never Reinforce Refusals

Refusals are occurrences in which the dog starts toward an obstacle then stops or turns back to you, as if he is unsure or has had second thoughts. From the very start of your training and throughout your dog's agility career, never accept or reward refusals. When commanding your dog to an obstacle, give only one command and expect the dog to comply.

Imagine that during a training session you send your dog to a tunnel. Your dog heads toward the tunnel and then, two feet from the opening, turns back to you as if to say, "Did you say tunnel?" You repeat your command emphatically — *Go tunnel! Go tunnel!* The dog eventually decides to enter the tunnel and you reward him when he exits. What has your dog just learned? He has learned that if he is not paying close attention and is not sure what you want him to do, he should stop or turn back to you and you will repeat your command. If he eventually complies, he will get a reward. Congratulations to your dog! He has trained you well. Not only is the dog now relieved of the burden of paying attention, he also has you trained to give him a treat for incurring refusals!

Refusals not only waste time but also are faulted in competition. To prevent refusals from becoming a permanent part of your dog's agility repertoire, address them head-on in your training sessions. When your dog incurs a refusal or runout, stop immediately. Give a verbal correction as soon as possible after the infraction. This helps communicate to your dog specifically what it was you did not like. To isolate and repair your problem, repeat only the portion of the sequence in which the dog made the mistake. Don't be tempted to add more obstacles to the front or end of the sequence! There is no justification whatsoever for this. If your dog makes a mistake on any of these extra obstacles, you will miss the opportunity to reward your dog for fixing his problem.

Give Your Command Before You Start Moving

If you start moving toward an obstacle before you give your dog a command, he is likely to start moving without a command. It is also quite likely that you will allow him to do this; you might even reward him for doing the obstacle! What, then, have you taught your dog? Your movement is now a cue to take the obstacle you appear to be moving toward — no verbal command is necessary. This may not seem to be a problem on a very simple course with limited options for the dog. Unfortunately, this can get you into big trouble in many other situations.

For example, when you want to lead out at the start line or from the table, you want your dog to stay in position until he is released on your verbal command. Another problematic situation is when your dog is approaching two obstacles placed very close together. If you have allowed him in the past to decide which obstacle to take based on which obstacle you appear to be moving toward — without any verbal command

— how can the dog be wrong if he chooses the tunnel instead of the dog walk? The answer is — he cannot be. What's more, if you tell him he is wrong, he will not understand why. You have changed the rules.

Your dog is not clairvoyant. It is impossible for him to know when you want him to take obstacles on your body movements alone and when you do not. Handlers who assume their dogs can read their minds often become upset and end up correcting the dogs for something for which they have rewarded their dogs in the past. These handlers are correcting their dogs for their own careless inconsistency! This can easily lead to attitude problems and a lack of trust in you as a team leader. As a result, your dog's speed and consistency can suffer.

The best answer is to never allow your dog to release himself from a stay or take an obstacle based on your body movements alone. Why would you ever want him to, anyway? When your commands are late? The obvious solution is to train yourself to give your commands on time! By being consistent with your rules, your dog always knows what to expect. He trusts you as a handler, and your training sessions and ring performances reflect true teamwork.

Keep Your Training Stress-Free and Fun

Your obstacle training sessions are the foundation for all of your future agility training. Get started on the right foot by making your obstacle-training sessions stress-free and fun. Your goal should be to make the dog feel wonderful for succeeding — even if he is only succeeding in small steps. Overly high expectations lead to stress on the part of the handler. Dogs can sense this stress and develop a poor attitude toward the sport before they have even given it a chance. Broken attitudes aren't easy to repair, so keep it light — even though you are dedicated to developing only good working habits.

Consistent Communication — Commands, Signals, and Body Language

Dogs determine the path you want them to take by interpreting your commands, signals, and body language. Using all three means of communication helps your dog understand your wishes. Although some dogs are more verbal than others, most dogs will follow your signals and body language when they conflict with your verbal commands. For example, if your signals and body language indicate the A-frame, but you give your verbal command for the tire instead, your dog would most likely perform the A-frame without hesitation. Verbal commands are very important, however, for instances in which the dog is ahead of you or working at a great distance from you. The farther away you are, the less of an impact your body language will have on your dog.

When your dog can interpret your wishes immediately without hesitation or uncertainty, he will have the best chance for a fast and smooth agility run. The key to instant communication is consistency. If you have trained your dog to respond to a set of commands, signals, and body language, and if you consistently use them in training and in the ring, your dog will know immediately what you want. The result will be fast and faultless rounds.

Signals

Some handlers you see in the ring use few, if any, signals. They choose instead to run alongside the obstacles with their elbows bent and arms swinging at their sides. Their dogs have been trained that this body posture means to take the obstacle that is nearest the handler. This established communication might be successful on a simple course or when the handler can run as fast as his dog. However, on more advanced courses, those in which the handler must take a path that is other than immediately alongside the obstacles, the communication breaks down. The dog is uncertain and mistakes occur.

To communicate with your dog most clearly, give a flat hand signal using the hand closest to your dog.

If you neglect to use signals, you are failing to take advantage of a very powerful communication tool that is available to you in the ring — free of charge! A good rule of thumb is that if doing something that helps your dog doesn't cost you anything (in terms of lost time, increased risk, etc.), why not do it? A signal helps you more clearly communicate what you want the dog to do.

Using signals along with your verbal commands during training gives your dog a consistent place on your body in which to seek direction. A signal can also be invaluable for directing your dog at a distance, as well as in noisy situations when it may be difficult to hear your verbal commands. Moreover, signals can sometimes compensate for late verbal commands.

To be effective, the signal must be consistent and clear to the dog. The best signals are firm, deliberate extensions of your arm held chest high or lower with your hand held flat.

(Pointed fingers are much more difficult to see than a flat hand!) The signaling hand should be raised into place and released smoothly to avoid distracting the dog. Frantic, choppy, or swinging signals can be distracting. They may draw the dog's attention to you rather than the upcoming obstacle. These also tend to twist your body, giving mixed signals to the dog about the path you want him to take.

Should you use signals even when the dog is ahead of you? Absolutely! The longer you participate in agility the more you will be convinced that your dog has eyes in the back of his head. The dog's superior peripheral vision and keen sense of where you are make it important that you continue with your signals and body language, regardless of what you think the dog can or cannot see.

Body Language

Many trainers, particularly those new to agility, fail to recognize the importance of the handler's body language in communicating direction to the dog. Once your dog learns a consistent set of body cues, you could eliminate verbal commands and your dog would most likely know where you wanted him to go.

Generally speaking, when you are working parallel to or facing the dog, your shoulders, pelvis, and feet should be facing the path you want the dog to take. When the dog is behind you, catching up with the back of you, you should be facing parallel to the path you want him to take. Much more will be discussed about body language in the chapters to follow, as it plays a very important role in sequencing and distance work.

Training Tools

To begin your obstacle training, you will need a **6-foot leather or nylon lead** and a tight-fitting **buckle collar**. For your dog's safety, do not use a choke chain or nylon choke collar. These collars can act like a noose and possibly damage the dog's trachea if they catch on something. If you need extra power-steering with a large or rambunctious dog, a prong (pinch) collar can be helpful. Despite its unfriendly appearance, a pinch collar does not choke the dog but applies firm, even pressure around the dog's neck.

When you progress to off-lead training, a 4-inch to 6-inch leather lead, called a **grab tab**, can be useful. The tab should be long enough to grab quickly but short enough so that it does not interfere with your dog's movement. For your dog's safety, use a knotted tab rather than a looped one. The loop could easily become caught on an obstacle.

You will also want to have a variety of **food treats** and/or **toys** available for use as an incentive (or lure) at first, then as an intermittent reward for good performance. The treats should be small enough for the dog to eat quickly without chewing. For some of your obstacle training it helps to use treats that will stick to surfaces. There are many commercial dog treats as well as acceptable human foods that meet this description. Experiment with a variety to see which work best for you and your dog.

While you are training, store your treats and/or toys in your pockets — not a waist pack or visible bait bag. If you always train with a visible treat-holder, when you enter the competition ring (where waist packs are prohibited) it will be obvious to your dog that no rewards will be forthcoming.

One of the most useful tools for encouraging your dog to work at a distance is a **target**. A good target for food-motivated dogs is a plastic margarine container lid with a small piece of food in the center. Placing the food on a visible target of this kind rather than directly on the ground prevents the dog from learning to sniff and root around for hidden food. When using a target, it is important to never allow the dog to cheat by rewarding himself without having performed the desired behavior. To prevent possible cheating you must have a very reliable recall. Alternatively, you could have a friend ready to cover the food and prevent the dog from rewarding himself should he attempt to cheat.

A multipurpose motivator that's especially useful for dogs that are not toy- or ball-oriented is a plastic **food container**. You can fill the container with treats and throw it as you would a toy or ball to encourage the dog to work ahead of you. When the dog touches the

container, you can run up, open the container, and give the dog a treat. Although you could throw food without a container, it is not advisable. The food is usually too small for the dog to see immediately and thus you would be encouraging the dog to spend time sniffing the ground looking for food.

For small dogs, you can use an empty film can — a small plastic container designed to hold a roll of photographic film. For larger dogs, it's safer and more visible to use a larger container. A good choice is a round, tennis-ball sized food storage container with a tight-fitting lid. Poking a few holes in the lid will release the scent of the food and make the container a more interesting chase object. If you fill the container with dry treats, you can shake it to make an attention-getting sound. If you prefer to reward with soft food, you can still use the container with the dry treats. When the dog runs to or retrieves the container, open the lid and pretend to get your soft treats from the container. Don't get lazy and reward from your pocket or your dog will soon learn to cut out the middleman and run to you instead of the container!

Besides throwing it, you can use your plastic container as a stationary closed target, similar to the way in which you would use a margarine container lid. Using this type of target is useful when you are training alone and do not want to risk having the dog reward himself for improper behavior.

For your obstacle training and for all of your agility training thereafter you will need a supply of **wire guides**. These tent-like training aids are indispensable for training weave poles, as well as for channeling your dog to the correct approach for all of the obstacles. You can also use them to keep your dog from running between the tire and the frame of the tire jump, and for blocking approaches to incorrect obstacles. Placing one or more of these guides over a jump bar can encourage your dog to pick up his feet as he jumps.

You can easily make a supply of guides by cutting and folding wire fencing material to the desired height and length. (Be sure to trim off any sharp edges!) The green-coated, very-small-mesh variety of fencing material called *hardware cloth* holds up particularly well over time and blends into the background of your training area.

For general use, guides that are 12 inches high and 2 to 3 feet in length are the most useful. You may also want to have a few giant-sized guides (2 feet high by 3 feet long) for large or rambunctious dogs that fail to see the purpose of the smaller ones.

If you have a tall or long-strided dog, you may want to have some **training hoops** available for your contact training. Training hoops help pattern the dog to lower his head and touch the upside and downside contacts of the dog walk, see-saw, and A-frame. Depending on your training area, you can use base-mounted or stick-in-the-ground hoops.

Racing through the closed tunnel is a blast! (Photo: Gene Abrahamson)

5 Tunnels and the Pause Table

Open Tunnel

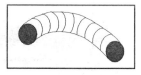 The open tunnel is an excellent place to begin your obstacle training program. Success is achieved quickly for the majority of dogs. The tunnels are safe for dogs of all ages and do not require a great amount of concentration on the part of the dog. What's more, tunnels are wonderful for early success at distance work.

For beginning training, you can buy a child's play tunnel or invest in a competition tunnel. The latter is much more expensive but will last for years and is also usable in competition.

PICTURE OF PERFECT PERFORMANCE

The dog runs at full speed to the correct entrance of the tunnel from any angle and exits quickly.

General Rules

The dog must enter the specified end of the tunnel and exit the other. Entering the correct end and then turning around and exiting through the entrance is scored as a refusal.

Commands

Choose a command for the open tunnel. Keep in mind that many old-timers to the sport selected the command *Tunnel!* for the open tunnel and *Table!* for the pause table, only to ruefully discover that those words sounded very much alike to the dog. At great distance and high speed, it can be even more difficult for the dog to tell these words apart. To avoid possible problems in your future training it would be wise to choose a command other than *Tunnel!* if you have your heart set on calling the table *"Table!"*

Step #1 — Recalls

For your first session, you will need to train with a helper. Start by compressing the tunnel to its shortest possible length.

With your dog on a six-foot (or longer) leather or nylon leash, have someone hold your dog as close as possible to the tunnel opening. Do not put the dog in a formal sit- or down-stay. If you do, he may break his stay as you move to the other side. If you ignore the break, you have compromised your stays. If you go back and enforce the stay command, you are taking valuable time from your training session and are making agility less fun for the dog.

Have your helper hold the dog steady at the tunnel opening. Go to the other side and have your helper throw the dog's leash through the tunnel to you. Take hold of the leash and establish friendly eye contact with your dog through the tunnel. With a reward ready in your opposite hand, give your tunnel command clearly and enthusiastically, tap the bottom edge of the tunnel and back up as the dog starts moving toward you.

When the dog exits the tunnel, praise and reward immediately with a treat or with a toy tossed a short distance.

DEALING WITH THE RELUCTANT DOG

If your dog is hesitant, you may need to crawl part way inside and show him a reward to entice him to come through on his own power. Couple this with lots of verbal encouragement. Do not try to pull him through the tunnel. Likewise, your helper should not try to push the dog through to you. This will only stimulate **opposition reflex**. This is a situation in which the dog applies the "brakes" to brace himself against attempts to push or pull him against his will. Pushing or pulling will result in a dog that is even more determined not to enter the tunnel. The helper may, however, position the dog's head so that he can see the handler through the tunnel opening rather than allowing him to look over the top for his owner.

> **TRAINING TIP:** *Never be tempted to throw anything into the tunnel. Chances are the thrown object will land inside, thus teaching your dog to sniff around and look for rewards inside the tunnel. Your goal is for the dog to run quickly through the tunnel — not dawdle inside. Therefore, the rewards should come only after the dog has quickly exited the other side!*

Step #2 — Run-Bys

When you are successful at calling your dog through a shortened tunnel, progress to a **run-by.** In a run-by, you will start in line with the dog (i.e., you will not lead out). You will direct the dog to the obstacle by giving its command and moving toward the path you want the dog to take. To help your dog be successful, your early run-bys will be on leash or using a tab.

Think about the path you will take toward the tunnel (Figure 5-1). If you and your dog were to start directly in front of the tunnel opening, and you both start moving toward it, you, the handler, will soon be forced to begin moving to the right to avoid running into the tunnel opening yourself. This means you will be turning your shoulder away from the path you want your dog to take. This can easily cause the dog to pull away from the tunnel with you (Figure 5-1, left panel). A much better solution is to position yourself to start slightly to the right of the tunnel opening with your path taking you on an angle toward the left (Figure 5-1, center panel). Alternatively, your dog could be set up in line with the tunnel opening (Figure 5-1, right panel). However, since you are holding your dog's lead or tab in these early stages of training, your dog will be required to start close by your side. Because of this, it is a good idea for both you and your dog to start slightly to the right of the tunnel opening.

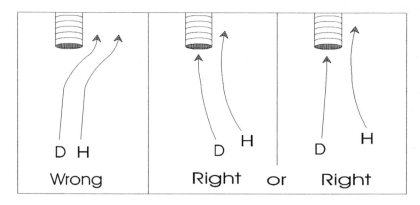

Figure 5-1: When beginning run-bys on the tunnel, choose a handling path that makes it easy for the dog to succeed. The dog is represented by "D" while "H" represents the handler.

Stand about eight feet away from and about five feet to the right of the shortened tunnel with the dog on leash at your left side. Hold the leash close to the collar for maximum control. Make sure your dog is looking at the tunnel. Give your command, then start moving toward the tunnel opening. Release the leash as the dog commits to the tunnel. If the dog balks at or runs around the tunnel at the last minute, go back to the tunnel recall until the dog is more confident. Then return to run-bys. Be sure to practice this step handling off both the right and the left.

Step # 3 — Increase Tunnel Length

Continue to perform run-bys, gradually increasing the length of the tunnel until it is fully extended. Next, put a slight bend in the tunnel. There should still be light visible to the dog from the other end of the tunnel. Gradually increase the amount of the curve until the dog is confident performing the tunnel when it is fashioned in a U-shape. When the tunnel is curved you will always take the inside, or shorter, path.

As the dog catches on, you will be able to release the leash or tab farther and farther away from the tunnel. Eventually, your dog will run toward and enter the tunnel entirely on his own, each time you give him a command.

Step #4 — Add Angles and Distance

Your next goal is to be able to call and send your dog to the tunnel from a variety of angles and distances. Ideally, you will gradually increase your distance until your dog is confident being called and sent to the tunnel on one command and signal from a distance of 30 feet. This is your first essential step in teaching the dog that you want him to work at his maximum speed — not hang back and try to match yours. The earlier in your training you can convey this, the better.

CALLING

To call your dog through the tunnel, start with a straight tunnel then progress to a slightly curved one. Place your dog in a sit-stay or have a friend hold him in position while you lead out to the other side of the obstacle. Start by positioning both you and your dog directly in line with the tunnel entrance and exit. As your dog gains confidence, increase the angle at which your dog must approach the tunnel, while you remain in line with the exit. Finally, vary your position as well as your dog's so that you can call him through a tunnel regardless of where either you or your dog is positioned.

TRAINING TIP: *When calling your dog from a sit-stay to an obstacle, do not preface the command with a release word, a* Come! *command, or the dog's name. Give only the command for the obstacle. Here's why:*

- *The **release word** releases the dog from working. It wastes time and does not convey what you want him to do. Moreover, he may decide what to do before you get the chance to issue your obstacle command.*

- *The* Come! *command is inappropriate since you do not want the dog to come toward you. You want him to travel in a direct line from his position to the obstacle, without veering toward you first. You will also use the* Come! *command to ask the dog to bypass obstacles, therefore confusion is likely to result.*

- ***Saying the dog's name** wastes time, and may serve to release the dog from his stay before you have the chance to give your obstacle command. It also relieves the dog of the burden of paying attention to you. You want the dog to take responsibility for watching you when you leave him on a stay or wait.*

SENDING

There are two basic ways to practice sending your dog to obstacles.

- You can leave your dog in a sit and lead out to a strategic handling position. We refer to this as an *offset start* because the obstacle to which you are sending the dog is offset from the path between you and your dog. You must therefore rely on your signal, verbal command, and body language to communicate the obstacle to be taken (Figure 5-2. The dashed arrows show the direction the handler should face, while the solid arrows show the dog's path.)

- You can send your dog from your side to an obstacle from various angles and distances, communicating with a signal, verbal command, and body language (Figure 5-3).

We refer to this as *on the fly* since the dog does not have to be placed in a sit before sending.

Both are skills that you and your dog need to master so be sure to practice them both while working on approaching from greater angles and larger distances.

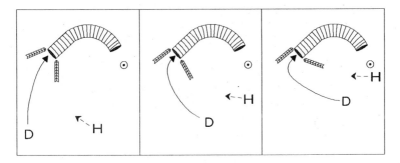

Figure 5-2: Sending to the tunnel using an "offset start."

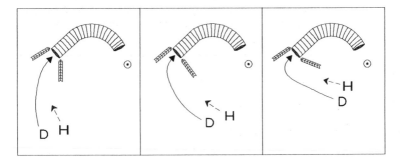

Figure 5-3: Sending the dog to the tunnel "on the fly."

Arrange the tunnel in a curved shape. You will be handling your dog from the inside of the arc, meaning the dog will take the longer running path rather than you. Set your dog up for success by using an incentive to encourage him to go ahead of you to the tunnel. This incentive could be a toy or food placed on a target about three feet from the tunnel exit. Alternatively, you could have someone squeak a toy and be ready to throw it as the dog exits.

Start by showing the dog the target or incentive without letting him reward himself. He now knows that something wonderful awaits him at the end of the tunnel.

For your first attempt, perform a run-by as you have in the past. As he exits (the moment his nose crosses the plane of the tunnel exit) release him to the target or toy with a command such as *Get it!* This release is important because you do not want to allow your dog to think that he is permitted to check out items of interest (anything that may appear to be edible or interesting to play with) while he is working with you on the course. He must wait until he has been released by you. This will become even more important when you begin planting distractions on the course for him to ignore.

Some dogs may bypass the tunnel and head straight for the target. This is to be expected. Prevent the dog from rewarding himself by covering the target and take steps to prevent him from bee-lining it to the target on the next attempt. This may require angling the tunnel exit somewhat so the target is not visible to the dog until he exits the tunnel. You could also use a barrier such as a ring gate or wire guides, or you could guide the dog by the leash or tab until he is committed to the tunnel. However you accomplish it, your dog will be rewarded for going through the tunnel. He will soon realize that rewards come only from obeying your obstacle command.

On subsequent tries, hang back more and more so that your dog is going a greater distance to the tunnel ahead of you. Be patient. Different dogs will progress at vastly different rates.

Gradually increase the angle of approach to the open tunnel. Start with mild angles, then progress to sending to the tunnel opening from 90-degree angles. Eventually, send at even greater angles, in which the tunnel opening is not visible. Your body language should indicate the correct path to take and will allow your dog to find the correct end of the tunnel. Wire guides can be helpful in preventing your dog from overshooting the tunnel opening. The guides serve as a funnel to channel him into the tunnel from a variety of angles.

CONCENTRATE ON BODY LANGUAGE

Your body language is extremely important when directing your dog to perform obstacles. In your early work with calling and sending you are building important cues, and will need to be very consistent in your communication with the dog. Keep in mind that you should be facing the path (or line) you want your dog to follow — not the next obstacle you want him to take. Facing the line helps eliminate any ambiguity about where you want your dog to go. The reason for this will be very obvious to you once you look at the situation from the dog's point of view.

Another way to help you think about facing the correct "line" is to think of the air between you and your dog as a clear, solid mass — like an ice cube! Alternatively, you could think of it as the air being a protective "force-field" or large "buffer zone." (Figures 5-4 and 5-5.) By pressing on the air in a specific direction you can influence your dog's path, keeping him from coming back toward you. When sending your dog to an obstacle, regardless of your starting position or your dog's, you will be pressing on the air toward a point roughly between where he started and where you want him to go.

If, in your training sessions, your dog doesn't take the path you intended, freeze! It's likely your feet are about to tattle on you. Look at the way they are facing. Your shoulders and pelvis are probably facing the same way, too. Are you facing between where the dog was and the obstacle you wanted him to take? If possible, have a friend put himself in your position so you can go to the dog's position and see what your body was telling him.

This entire concept of the handler's path may sound strange at first, but don't dismiss this as voodoo until you've tried it! Do some experiments of your own to see what the dog sees when you face the line and when you don't.

A dog's eye view: The handler is facing the correct end of the tunnel. Can you tell for certain which one it is?

The handler is facing the line she wants the dog to take. Is there less uncertainty now?

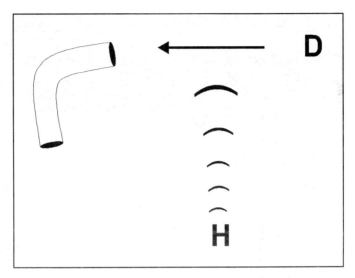

Figure 5-4: Think of the air between you and your dog as a solid. Pressing toward the dog's path helps propel him in the correct direction.

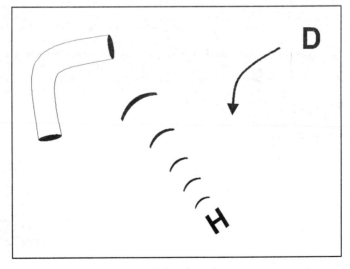

Figure 5-5: Pressing toward the obstacle creates uncertainty about the path the you want the dog to take and does nothing to propel him in the correct direction.

KEEP YOUR MOVEMENTS SMOOTH

In addition to facing in the correct direction to communicate with your dog, you also need to be concerned about the technique of your movements. Even a perfect handling strategy will fail if it is not executed properly.

When you are sending your dog, start at least 15 feet from the obstacle you want him to take. Give your command and signal and take several small steps to give your dog the line. Then, come to a smooth, gliding halt, stopping with one foot ahead of the other. When you have stopped moving, you should still be facing the direction you want the dog to go. Your shoulders, feet, and pelvis should all be facing the line.

Stopping abruptly can take your dog "off the line." Think of what would happen if you were to run full-speed with long strides up to a line and then stop abruptly. Once your feet stopped, your upper body would most likely rotate and then straighten out. This "planting and twisting" maneuver can easily pull your dog off the line. Dogs have excellent peripheral vision that is almost like having eyes in the back of their head. They can feel when your shoulder turns or when you stop abruptly — even if you are behind them.

If you are one of those lucky, long-legged athletic types, you will need to train yourself to take small steps when needed, rather than taking large steps and then stopping or turning away. The farther back you start from the obstacle, the easier this is to accomplish.

NEVER ACCEPT REFUSALS

Be sure not to build in refusals. **Give only one command** for the tunnel. If the dog stops before entering the tunnel, he has incurred a refusal and has not met your high standards. Immediately give your verbal correction (e.g., *Uh-oh! Oops! or Wrong!)* and break off the exercise. If you give him additional commands and allow him to continue, you have just taught your dog to rely on additional commands. We want the dog to act on the first command without seeking reassurance. Make it easier to succeed on the next try by shortening the distance and/or providing a bigger incentive.

Closed (Collapsed) Tunnel

Once the dog has achieved success with the open tunnel, the closed tunnel is easy to master.

PICTURE OF PERFECT PERFORMANCE

The dog runs at full speed to the entrance of the tunnel from any angle. As he enters the chute, he pushes through quickly in a straight line without veering or jumping upward. The dog then exits straight ahead without curling back.

General Rules

The dog must enter through the rigid opening and exit in a straight line through the chute. Entering and then turning around and exiting through the entrance is scored as a refusal.

Commands

The command you use can be the same as the one you have chosen for the open tunnel, or a different command, such as *Chute!* The closed tunnel and the open tunnel can look very similar to the dog from a head-on approach. From a side view, however, the closed tunnel does have a very different appearance. For this reason, it is a good idea to use a different command for each of the two types of tunnels.

Step #1 — Recalls

Start by using the rigid part of the closed tunnel, without the chute attached. Make sure that it is heavily weighted or firmly anchored to the ground so that the obstacle will not move when a dog runs through it.

Begin exactly the same way you did when introducing the open tunnel. Have your helper hold the dog in front of the tunnel opening and throw your leash through. Go to the other side, take the leash and establish friendly eye contact with your dog through the tunnel. Give your command, step backwards, praise, and reward.

To begin training the closed tunnel, start with recalls through the rigid opening only.

Step #2 — Run-Bys

With the chute still unattached, progress to run-bys off both the right and the left as described for the open tunnel. When proficient, attach the fabric chute. Roll it back completely, so it extends as little as possible past the rigid portion. Have your dog perform run-bys off both your left and right sides. To progress further, you will need an assistant.

Each time your dog performs a successful run-by, have your assistant extend the chute an additional foot or so while holding it as wide open as possible. As the dog gains confidence, you will be able to drop the leash earlier and earlier as you approach the obstacle. As with all obstacles, if at any time you encounter a problem, back up one or more steps.

> **TRAINING TIP:** *In a class situation, if a dog develops a confidence problem and shows reluctance to attempt the obstacle, don't let the other dogs watch! Any fear can be easily transmitted to the others, making them more likely to be reluctant when it is their turn to try.*

When your dog is confidently performing the collapsed tunnel with the chute fully extended but held wide open, have your assistant begin to close it partially, so the dog will feel the fabric on his back. Progress to holding the chute almost closed, merely applying tension at the end. Then, have the dog perform the obstacle with no help at all from you or your assistant.

AVOIDING THE TANGLES

Always make sure the chute is smooth and straight before each repetition or the dog may become entangled. At some time in your dog's agility career he inevitably *will* become entangled in the chute — despite your best efforts to ensure that the chute has been straightened beforehand. Help the dog immediately by grasping and straightening the end of the chute but don't panic and don't baby him! Fawning over your "poor little baby" can lead to him developing a fear of the closed tunnel, since you have reinforced him for being scared. Your dog could also come to the conclusion that wrapping himself up in the chute was really fun — after all, everyone showered him with attention! Often the dog himself is responsible for causing the tangle. You definitely do not want to reinforce this behavior. Help him escape and re-approach the obstacle right away. You may have to hold the chute fully open to get him to try again.

RUNNING STRAIGHT THROUGH THE CHUTE

Our picture of perfect performance calls for the dog to run straight through the chute with all energy expended in a forward direction. Dogs sometimes stray from this ideal in several ways:

- **Dog jumps upward before exiting.** This can cause the dog to become entangled. At the very least, it delays the dog from exiting the chute, which wastes time. If you notice this happening, take immediate steps to prevent this behavior from becoming a habit. Hold the chute fully extended, but open so there will be no incentive to jump up. Throw a ball as the dog exits, or place a target several feet from the exit to encourage the dog to drive forward rather than upward. When the dog is no longer jumping, gradually begin to lower the chute again, keeping a close watch on his technique.

  If your dog is well beyond the learning stages and has already developed this habit, you may need to retrain using the steps described above. Alternatively, you could try holding a PVC pole parallel to the ground above the chute at the point at which the dog begins to jump. It should be held high enough so that if the dog does not jump, there will be no contact between the dog and the pole.

- **Dog arcs to one side while pushing through the chute.** Like the problem above, arcing can also waste time and cause the dog to become entangled and/or can waste time on the course. Make sure you don't contribute to this problem by handling primarily off one side. You can also inadvertently cause this problem if you habitually send your dog through the tunnel while remaining at the entrance, and then call the dog back to you after he exits. It is easy for your dog to develop the habit of turning back to you as soon as he exits the chute — or worse yet, starting to head back to you while he is still pushing through the chute. To avoid these problems, make an effort to be even with or ahead of your dog as he exits the chute when initially teaching the obstacle. If your dog is very fast, this may require having someone hold and launch him while you lead out for a head start.

Steps # 4 and 5 — Add Distance and Angles

Progress to calling and sending to the closed tunnel as you did with the open tunnel, with increasingly more difficult angles and distances.

Step #6 — Add Moisture

Don't consider the closed tunnel fully trained until you have taught your dog to perform it with a wet chute. Agility trials are held in all types of weather. Even a three-pound Chihuahua is required to push through a soaking wet chute during a rainstorm. To train for wet conditions, start slowly. Use a spray bottle to dampen the chute slightly. Reinforce good performance with extra-special rewards. When the dog has overcome any aversion to a damp chute, progress to a soaking wet one.

Pause Table

THE PICTURE OF PERFECT PERFORMANCE

The dog leaps onto the table quickly, smoothly, without hesitation, and without sliding or jumping off the opposite side. Upon hearing the handler's command to down or sit (which is given no later than the instant all four feet touch the table top) the dog complies swiftly and focuses keen attention on the handler, awaiting his next command. As the judge counts down for five seconds, the dog remains firmly planted in the desired position on the table while the handler moves swiftly to an advantageous lead-out position. The dog springs from the table immediately when the handler issues one of the following: an obstacle command for the next obstacle to be performed, a directional command such as *Come!* or *Out!*, or a release word such as *OK* if the training exercise is finished. The dog is never released on the handler's body motions, praise, or an informal command.

General Rules

The dog must jump on the table and assume the specified position (sit or down) for five seconds. A typical count by the judge is *Five, Four, Three, Two, One, Go!*

Dogs are faulted for jumping or sliding off the table before the five seconds have elapsed. If the dog leaves the table a fraction of a second too early, he is faulted for anticipating the count.

If the dog breaks his position on the table but does not jump off, no faults are assessed, however, time is lost while the handler repositions his dog. In most types of competition, the table count is consecutive, that is, if the dog breaks position, the judge starts his count over from the beginning when the dog is back in position. In others, the count is cumulative; the judge resumes counting where he left off when the dog broke his position.

Commands

Choose a command that is unique to the table. The command will mean "find the table and quickly jump on it." Don't choose the same command as one you might use for your grooming table or the command you use to ask your dog to jump on your bed. The commands *Bench!, Rest!* or *Pause!* are all good choices. If you decide to use the command *Table!*, think twice about choosing *Tunnel!*. Try *Through!* instead.

Step #1 — Jumping Onto the Table

To make it easy for your dog to be successful, start with a low table. With your dog on a leash on your left side, start about 6 - 8 feet from the table, approaching at a slight angle from the right. Focus your dog's attention on the obstacle. Give your command then move toward it, tapping the table top with your hand. Use encouragement if necessary, but don't repeat your table command. In most cases, the dog will be happy to comply; after all, jumping on furniture is something most dogs enjoy! If your dog is reluctant, you may find it helpful to jump on the table with him until he realizes it is a desirable place to be.

When the dog has jumped on the table, pet, praise, and then release using a **release word** such as *OK!* or *Free!* A release word discharges the dog from the previous command, and signifies that he is off-duty, at least temporarily. Remember to work off both sides and do not accept or reward refusals. As soon as the dog catches on, eliminate tapping the top of the table with your hand, as this will not be permitted in competition.

Step #2 — Adding the Sit or Down

To progress any further your dog must know how to down and/or sit on command. (Some forms of agility require only a down on the table.) The dog should comply reliably on one command and/or signal, on a variety of surfaces (wet grass, damp concrete, gravel, pine needles, mud, etc.), and with a variety of visual and audible distractions. Only then should you expect your dog to sit and down on the pause table. For the best results, you should train these commands away from the time and place you train agility. If you don't, you risk causing the dog to form a bad attitude toward the table or toward agility in general.

If you haven't already trained a reliable sit, stay, down, and come, consult one the many excellent books and videos available on obedience training. Better yet, enroll in an obedience class. You will enjoy the benefits of expert guidance, while training among the distractions of other dogs and people.

With your dog on-lead, give your command for the table and run toward it with him. At the moment all four of your dog's feet touch the table top, give your command to sit or down. Don't use the dog's name before the command. This provides no useful information and only delays your command to sit or down. Remember, every fraction of a second counts!

If the dog does not comply on your first command, **don't repeat your command!** Instead, help him by gently moving him into position or by luring him with food. Repeating your command to sit or down sets a terrible precedent and is a sure way of setting yourself up for future problems in the ring. Repeating your command is essentially begging and communicates to your dog that he is in charge and that complying is purely optional. What you will get as a result in the ring is a dog that ignores repeated commands to sit or down until the handler is screaming in frustration. Even then, the dog might decide not to cooperate.

If you've been a spectator at agility trials, no doubt you have seen some desperate handlers who beg and plead with their dogs to down or sit on the table while the seconds tick away. A very memorable illustration of this occurred at a trial in which a handler had a stand-off with her 90-pound Rottweiler. The Rottie just didn't want to lie down on the table. After repeated and insistent begging, and what seemed like an eternity of elapsed time, the handler turned to the audience and asked, "has anybody got a gun?" The dog did not ever decide to lie down. You can help make sure this never happens to you by making a habit of giving your commands only once during training, and then enforcing them if your dog does not comply.

USING SIT OR DOWN SIGNALS

In the competition ring, you are permitted to use any number and type of commands and/or signals to communicate with your dog — as long as they are in good taste (i.e., not obscene or threatening). Since you can use signals as well as verbal commands, it makes sense to use both for the pause table. This is extra communication with your dog that costs you nothing. To make your wishes clear to the dog in the most immediate fashion, use your right hand for your *Down!* signal and your left hand for your *Sit!* signal.

Give your command and signal to sit or down the moment all four feet touch the table top.

MAINTAINING THE POSITION

After the dog is in the sit or down position on the table, command him to *Stay!* or *Wait!,* then take a step or two backwards. If he breaks his position, give an immediate verbal correction, then place him back into position. Remind him to stay — once. Move away again, but not quite as far as you did the first time. You want the dog to be successful. If he is, tell him *Good stay!* and return to him and reward. Then release. If he is not, place him back into position and make it even easier to succeed on the next try.

> **TRAINING TIP:** *When you are working on getting your dog to remain steady in a sit or down position, never reward the release. Instead, reward when he is in the position you are asking for. If you reward the release he will be anxious to break his stay to earn his treat. Rewarding him in the position you want makes him content to stay where you left him until the treat is delivered.*

Step #3 — Reinforcing the Stay

At an agility trial, your dog will need to maintain a rock-steady position on the table in spite of any number of tempting distractions. If your dog has never been taught to ignore all distractions and maintain his position, you cannot expect him to be reliable in the competition ring.

The following are some ideas for reinforcing the stay. In all cases, praise and reward for staying. Then release. If the dog breaks his stay, give a timely verbal correction and repeat the exercise, making it easier to succeed on the next try.

With the dog in the desired position on the pause table,

- Attach a leash and apply gentle pressure. The dog should brace against the leash tension if he understands that he must stay.

- Make a sudden movement away from the table. As the dog learns what is expected and catches on to the game, make the movements progressively more sudden and dramatic.

- Hold a treat or toy above the dog's head or in front of his nose.

- Toss a toy or treat-filled food container a short distance away.

- Have a friend play the part of the judge by counting and saying an enthusiastic "*GO!*"

AVOID HOVERING

Be careful not to hover over the pause table to get your dog to stay. You will inadvertently be training him that he must stay in position only as long as you are leaning over him in a threatening manner. This makes you a slave to the table, preventing you from leading out. What's more, you are so close to your dog that any slight movement on your part may cause him to move. You are forced to stand as still as a statue until the count is finished. When you *do* start moving, your dog is likely to start moving as well — regardless of any command you may or may not have given.

Because hovering prevents you from leading out, you are often in a poor position to indicate to your dog which obstacle is next. The resulting confusion can, at the very least, cause wasted time from head checks and spins. It can also result in refusal or wrong course faults as your dog tries so second-guess you about the next obstacle.

A dog's eye view: The handler is hovering over the dog on the table. Can the dog tell which obstacle will follow the table?

A dog's eye view: The handler leads out while the judge performs the table count. Is it more obvious where the dog will be going next?

RELEASE FROM THE TABLE

To release your dog from his position in the table, use your release word. (This will only be the case when the table is at the end of a sequence or when training the table as an individual obstacle. When performing another obstacle after the table, use an obstacle or directional command to release your dog from the table.) Your dog should never be released by praise. Why?

Because you will want to be able to praise your dog for a fast sit or down without releasing him from his position. Likewise, you should never release your dog on a body movement. You will want to be able to move freely while the dog remains stationary on the table.

> **TRAINING TIP:** *Be careful not to habitually couple your release command with a concurrent body movement. You may unwittingly teach your dog that a quick movement away from the table is a release. To prevent any association between your release and your body movement, vary your position when releasing. Sometimes release while you are moving, and sometimes release while you are stationary. Occasionally, you can even release the dog concurrent with the start of a body movement.*

INCREASING LEAD-OUT DISTANCE

As soon as your dog is steady in position on the table with distractions present and without your hovering over him, start to increase the distance you lead out from the table. At first, move away from the table slowly. If he is steady, return to him and praise/reward while he is still in position. If he breaks, give a timely verbal correction and place him back into position. Gradually progress to being able to run away from the table quickly and suddenly while the dog maintains his stay.

INSIST ON ATTENTION

The entire time your dog is in position on the table he should be looking at you attentively. Why? When you begin sequencing, you will be releasing the dog using your command for the next obstacle. If the dog is looking elsewhere, you will have to waste precious seconds getting his attention before giving your command.

Step #4 — Sending to the Pause Table

Your next goal is to be able to send your dog to the table from gradually increasing distances.

Set your dog up for success by placing a toy or target on the table. Position the target toward the back of the table top so that the dog will have to jump on the table to get the reward. Show him the incentive but don't let him have it.

Start with the dog at your side about 15 feet from a low table. Use a tab attached to the dog's collar instead of a leash. Focus his attention ahead to the table, give your command and begin moving toward it. Instead of going all the way to the table with him, hang back somewhat without coming to an abrupt stop. The dog will most likely continue to the table and jump on it. When he does, immediately command *Get it!* to release him to the target. Releasing to the target releases the dog from the exercise. Do not ask him to sit or down.

If he does not get on the table on your first command, break off the exercise. He did not meet your high standards. Repeating your command will only serve to reinforce refusals. Make it easier to succeed without a refusal next time by shortening the distance to the table, showing him a bigger or better incentive, or revving the dog up with your voice. Restrained recalls also work well to increase motivation. Have someone hold your dog back as you excite him and point out the target. A few dogs do not pull when they are restrained. For these you may try launching them with a pop in the desired direction using your tab.

> **TRAINING TIP:** *When training your dog to send to obstacles, any distracting movement or sound on your part can distract the dog and cause him to turn back to you. When hanging back make sure you do not stop too abruptly. Your goal is to come to a smooth, gliding halt that does not draw the dog's attention. When you stop, your body should be facing the direction you want your dog to go, one foot ahead of the other, with your signal still extended or gradually withdrawn.*

Gradually increase the distance at which you send to the table, and gradually decrease the number of steps you take with him. Eventually you should be able to send the dog on one command from a distance of 30 - 40 feet, taking only one or two steps to give the dog a line.

PRACTICING WITH DIFFERENT SURFACES

Pause tables come with a variety surfaces — Astroturf, carpeting, rubber matting, and textured sand paint, to name a few. Try to get access to many different types of tables so your dog will have no surprises in the ring. If no other tables are available, change the look and feel of your existing tables by strapping on temporary surfaces. Add-on materials that work well include sheets of corrugated plastic or cardboard; or sheets of fabric such as towels, sheets, or blankets.

Step #6 — Adding Moisture

Always keep in mind that agility is an all-weather sport. You cannot consider the pause table mastered until your dog will perform perfectly on a table that is soaking wet. A prerequisite to this is for your dog to be reliable on the sit and down on a variety of surfaces with a variety of distractions. Start gradually by lightly dampening the table with a spray bottle. Then progress to a soaking wet one. At no time should you ever allow sniffing or slow responses to your down and sit commands. Rewarding these behaviors can cause your dog to think that this is the way you want him to do agility!

6 Weave Poles

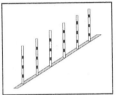 Superior weave pole skills are often what separate mediocrity from magnificence in the agility ring. If you have a few minutes available for some spur-of-the moment agility training, spending that time on your dog's weave pole skills will often give you a great return on your training investment.

Your dog's accuracy, speed, and independence on the weave poles are crucial to your success in the agility ring. The weave poles are arguably the most faulted obstacle. What's more, poor weave pole skills are responsible for many valuable seconds lost on the course.

The next time you attend an agility trial, watch for differences in the dogs' techniques as they perform the weave poles. Some dogs are painfully slow while others are lightning fast. The lightning fast ones seem to be having more fun, and, not surprisingly, so do their handlers!

Look at the dogs' *head positions*. The slower, less accurate dogs tend to be looking down at the ground, up at their handlers, or away to the side as if distracted. Their eyes are often looking everywhere but straight ahead, which is where you want them to go! How can they move forward at full speed if they are not looking forward? They can't! The faster-weaving dogs tend to focus directly ahead, driving in a forward direction. Their footwork is the most efficient possible for their size and structure. With this in mind, we can describe a mental picture of perfect performance.

PICTURE OF PERFECT PERFORMANCE

The dog enters the poles correctly to the right of the first pole without handler assistance — at top speed and from any angle. The dog continues to weave at lightning speed and without missing a pole, regardless of the handler's position or the distance from his dog. Throughout the process, the dog's head remains focused straight ahead. The footwork he uses is the most efficient for his size and structure, hugging the center line of the poles as closely as possible. The dog exits quickly and accurately, regardless of the handler's movements or position.

Superior weave pole skills are often what separate mediocrity from magnificence in the agility ring. (Photo: Bill Newcomb)

General Rules

The dog must enter to the right of the first weave pole and continue without missing a pole. Missed entries and missed poles may be faulted. Failure to correct missed poles or missed entries results in a penalty for failure to perform.

Training Methods — A Comparative Overview

There are almost as many techniques for training the weave poles as there are trainers — and all enjoy a degree of success. There is no one best way to train weave poles, particularly if you are training on our own. You may even want to try a combination of methods. For each method in use, you will find dogs that weave spectacularly, dogs that weave miserably, and dogs that fall somewhere between the two extremes. The degree of success you can achieve depends largely on the trainer, and what his expectations are of the dog. An excellent trainer can achieve success with any method, provided he is observant and sets his standards high from the onset of his dog's weave pole training.

BUMP AND GRIND

In the early days of agility in the U.S., the bump and grind (or push/pull) was the predominant weave pole training method. Rather than using a special set of training poles to make it easier for the dog to succeed and to develop efficient footwork, this method starts immediately with regulation weave poles. The handler guides his dog in and out through the series of upright poles using his collar and leash, and sometimes hip movement.

Advantages:

- Requires no special equipment.

- No transition is necessary from training equipment to competition equipment.

Disadvantages:

- Very easy for dog to develop poor footwork and head position, since the most common and natural path through the upright poles is a loose, s-type pattern. This usually results in slow performance.

- Very easy for the dog to make a mistake by missing a pole or an entry.

- Dog can form an aversion to the obstacle if the trainer finds it necessary to drag or pull him through. This can also result in slow performance.

Regulation weave poles.

CHANNEL (CHUTE) METHOD WITH WIRES OR FENCES

A channel is made by moving all of the odd-numbered poles to the right a certain amount. Wires connect all the odd poles and all the even poles to prevent the dog from leaving the chute before all poles are performed. At first, the channel is made wide enough so that the dog can run down the center without weaving much at all. As the dog progresses, the chute is made narrower and the dog is required to "weave" more to negotiate the chute of poles.

Weave pole chute with wires.

Some trainers prefer to use fences (panels made of chicken wire, hardware cloth, or flexible snow fencing) instead of wires. These prevent the dog from ducking under or jumping over the wires to escape the chute.

Gradually the wires or fences are removed until the dog is weaving on his own.

Advantages:

- Dog is prevented from making a mistake, so his attitude and speed are good from the start.

- Independent weaving is learned from the start.

- Training equipment for this method is available commercially.

Disadvantages:

- Can be problematic for use in class since the height of the wires and the width of the chute may need to be adjusted for different dogs. Since this is time-consuming, it is often neglected. If you do not set the wires at precisely the right height, the dog may be tempted to jump over them or duck under them. You may also need to add or remove wires to accommodate dogs at various stages of their training.

- Dogs often have difficulty transitioning between wires and no wires (or fences and no fences).

- Some dogs, especially those without a great deal of drive, may develop poor footwork and head position.

- Some dogs develop an overly loose weaving style. By throwing their bodies outward until they hit a barrier, they learn to negotiate the poles in a pronounced zigzag pattern. What can result is a dog that blows out of the poles when the barriers are removed.

SLANTED POLE METHOD

With this method, regulation-length poles are slanted in an alternating pattern in a V-shaped configuration, so that it is easy for dogs to weave without errors. As a dog progresses, the poles are gradually raised until they are in the fully upright competition configuration.

Advantages:

- Dog is prevented from making a mistake, so his attitude and speed are good from the start.

- Independent weaving is learned from the start.

- Training equipment for this method is available commercially or can be made easily and inexpensively.

Disadvantages:

- Some dogs learn an inefficient weaving style, expending excess energy upward by trying to hop over the poles rather than weave through them.

- Can be difficult to transition from slightly slanted to fully upright poles.

- Some dogs, particularly those without a great deal of drive, may develop poor footwork and head position.

- Can be problematic for use in class, since individual students will be at different stages of slant. To adjust the poles properly for each dog is time consuming, so it is often neglected.

Slanted poles.

FLASHPAWS OFFSET POLE METHOD

The method employed in FlashPaws training classes is unique from the above methods in several ways. Our goal was to devise a method that would focus on developing the most efficient head position and footwork from the start, while teaching the dog to expend all energy in a forward direction. We also needed a method that was practical for class use, as well as for students to use at home. The result — the FlashPaws offset weave-pole method, which is described in the pages that follow.

FlashPaws offset weave poles.

Advantages:

- Training equipment for using this method can be made easily and inexpensively.

- Concentrates on most efficient footwork and head position from start.

- In most cases, dogs have little difficulty transitioning to competition poles.

- Dogs learn to drive forward and use their muscles to hug the center line, optimizing the dog's speed through the poles.

- The dog learns to use the most efficient footwork and head position from the start, so no retraining is necessary.

- No gradual adjustments of the equipment are necessary. In a group setting, all students use the same equipment setup, which maximizes the time available for weave pole training.

- Dogs acquire high-level weave pole skills relatively quickly — many in just a few months.

Disadvantages:

- Requires the trainer to be an integral, active, thinking part of the process from the start.

- The dog learns weaving independence only after the dog learns the proper technique.

Weave Pole Training Procedures — FlashPaws Offset Weave Pole Method

This method begins with a set of 5 or 6 short, offset weave poles. The poles are offset 1-1/2 inches from a center line (or 3 inches from pole to pole) and are spaced 20″ apart. The poles themselves are shorter than regulation poles. Our offset poles are 30 inches tall, rather than the typical 39-inch regulation poles. The poles may be stuck in the ground or permanently mounted in a base. It is important that the poles have some degree of flexibility to assist in developing the proper footwork and attitude from the start.

Base-mounted poles are the most convenient for moving around your training area. Industrial springs are a good choice for constructing pole supports. They make the poles flexible, safe, and durable.

It is possible to purchase commercial metal bases that are adjustable for the amount of offset you desire. (This is often the same base that you can use for the channel and wires method). These bases are generally rigid, however. To make them suitable for early weave pole training, you can use flexible plastic electrical conduit instead of PVC. In doing so, the bases will not flex but the poles will.

Stick-in-the-ground poles are an economical alternative to base-mounted poles. The disadvantages are that they cannot be moved around easily, and the poles soon become loose and slanted. This usually requires you to move the poles to another location. (The deeper you drive the stakes into the ground, the more stable your poles will become.) To construct a set of stick-in-the-ground poles, use garden stakes or rebar and drive them into the ground using a hammer. Then cover the stakes with PVC poles cut to a length of 30 inches. If you are using stick-in-the-ground poles, it's best to have at least 12 poles on hand. If you prefer to use poles that are mounted on a base, acquire two sets of five or six poles.

To train the weave poles, you will also need at least four wire guides, as described in Chapter 4.

Commands

Before beginning to teach the weave poles, decide what command you will use. *Weave!* or *Poles!* are good choices. You sometimes hear handlers use a two-word command such as *In-Out!* each time the dog is supposed to weave in and out of the poles. This is a poor choice for many reasons: You may become confused and tell your dog *out* when you want him to go *In.* More importantly, you eventually want the dog to sail through the poles much faster than you can possibly *say In-*

Out-In-Out-In-Out! Also, when you are calling or sending your dog through the weave poles, what constitutes *in* or *out?*

Step #1 — Introduction to the Offset Poles

Start with a set or five or six offset poles.

> **TRAINING TIP:** *Keep in mind that when you use an odd-numbered set of offset poles you can only approach them from one direction. If you approach from the wrong direction you will be teaching your dog to enter to the left of the first pole!*

Your dog should be on-leash (small dogs) or wearing a grab tab (large dogs) with a tight-fitting buckle collar. Standing about three feet from the entry to the weave poles, position your dog at your left side. Gather all excess leash in your left hand.

Place a highly motivational incentive such as liver or other wonderful treat or toy in your right hand. Focus the dog's attention ahead toward the weave poles. Give your command to weave, then move toward the entrance. Make sure you give your dog the straightest possible approach to the entrance to make it easy for him to be successful.

CONCENTRATE ON TECHNIQUE

Lure the dog straight through the center line of the poles by placing the incentive directly in front of his nose with your right hand. Your goal is to keep the dog driving forward and to keep his head looking straight ahead at all times. To encourage the dog to drive forward, pull backward (not upward) with the leash or tab in your left hand so that he must pull forward to reach toward the incentive. If he looks down at the ground, away to the side, or up at you, stop immediately. Bring the incentive closer to the dog's nose to regain his focus ahead and continue to weave.

Another equally important goal is to draw the dog through the poles hugging the center line as closely as possible. To encourage the most efficient footwork, avoid allowing the dog to take a wild Z-shaped or loose S-shaped path through the poles. You can help him achieve this by moving your hand with the incentive in as straight a line as possible (Figure 6–1). Use only a slight flick of your wrist rather than a dramatic zig-zag when luring the dog through the poles.

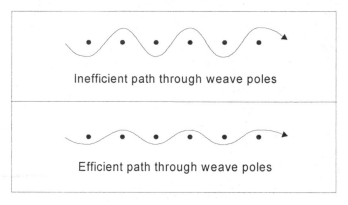

Figure 6-1: For the fastest and most efficient weave-pole performance, train your dog to hug the center line of the poles.

Make sure that you bring the armpit of your luring arm completely and smoothly over the top of the poles so that you are not raising and lowering your hand as the dog weaves. (This is why the poles are kept short!) If this is difficult for you, as it can be with small dogs or for people with back problems, you may find it helpful to use a dowel to hold your incentive. Place a sticky treat such as peanut butter on the end of the dowel. Alternatively, you can attach a small toy to the end of the dowel using Velcro. In class, we use dowels with an alligator clip attached to the end (a **clip stick**). This allows the handler to attach whatever incentive the dog prefers.

Step #1: Training the weave poles.

Using the dowel as an extension of your arm, move it in a very controlled manner as you move down the center line of the poles. Be careful not to move the dowel in a zig-zag path.

Reward and praise profusely when the dog exits. As he gains proficiency, you can begin to hold the incentive farther away from his nose, until it is one pole ahead of the dog. As you progress, if at any time you lose the dog's forward attention and proper head position, stop. Bring the incentive in closer and continue weaving.

> **TRAINING TIP:** *Make sure you move alongside your dog, facing the same direction he is going. Do not walk backwards as you lure your dog. Moving in a forward direction helps ease the transition as you begin to remove your training aids.*

Step #1: Training the weave poles using a dowel or clip stick.

DEALING WITH THE RELUCTANT DOG

A few dogs may be reluctant to brush their bodies against the plastic poles or to walk across the weave pole base. Avoid dragging or pulling a reluctant dog. This will usually lead to him putting on the brakes (also called *opposition reflex*), causing him to be more reluctant than ever to cooperate. Instead, use a more powerful incentive or start with a hungrier dog. It may also help to step across the line of poles with the dog for the first few attempts. For dogs who are concerned about stepping on the base, try starting with stick-in-the-ground weave poles and then progressing to base-mounted ones.

If your dog is one of the hesitant ones, don't despair. With time and patience he will eventually overcome all resistance and learn to love sailing through the weave poles.

WEAVING OFF BOTH SIDES FROM THE START

Don't even think about weaving only off the left! To be truly competitive, your dog *must* be able to weave equally well off both your right and your left. If you work your dog off both sides from the start, his skills will be equally strong from either side of you. As a result you will be confident and prepared for either eventuality from the day you begin to compete.

Step #2 — Eliminating the Leash

When you can hold your incentive a pole ahead of the dog without losing his head position and forward attention, and without missing any poles, you are ready to try eliminating the leash or tab. For some dogs this stage will come after only a few sessions. For others, it may mean spending a month or more acclimating the dog to the obstacle. Most dogs are ready for Step #2 within two to three weeks.

Remove your dog's leash or tab and transfer the incentive to your left hand. With your dog on your left side, give your command and approach the poles as before. (If your dog is fast, it may help to place him in a sit-stay or have a friend hold him in position while you get slightly ahead.) Have the dog follow your hand with the incentive straight through the center line of the poles. You will probably have to move the incentive back to a position near the dog's nose.

Don't push for speed when the you first remove the leash. Maintaining accuracy, footwork, and head position are much more important at this stage. Remaining calm with your tone of voice will help keep your dog from missing poles. Wire guides can also help keep the dog from making a mistake. If, despite all of your efforts, the dog is still missing poles, he is not ready to progress to the off-lead stage.

Be sure to work off the right just as often as you work off the left!

Step #2: Eliminating the leash or tab.

Step #3 — Eliminating the Lure

When your dog is weaving well off-leash with an incentive, place the reward in your pocket. Guide the dog with your hand as you did when you were using the lure. Praise lavishly and produce the reward from your pocket when he exits. Progress to rewarding intermittently for perfect and/or improved performances.

Gradually eliminate the use of your hand until your dog is weaving without any guidance from you.

If needed, use wire guides to channel the dog to enter or exit correctly, or to prevent him from skipping a particular pole.

Step #3: Eliminating the use of your hand as a lure.

INTRODUCING YOUR DOG TO THE WIRE GUIDES

The first time you use wire guides in your weave pole training, you will need to introduce them to your dog. At first, he will not understand what they are used for. Some dogs display initial fear and avoid getting near them. Others plow them down or jump over them without a care.

When confronted with these reactions, some handlers decide immediately that their dog doesn't like wire so they will not use the guides. Congratulations! Those dogs have trained their handlers well, but to their own detriment. Guides are your dog's friends. They help him be correct and receive more rewards.

Through patience and repetition you can show your dog there is nothing to fear. You can also teach him not to jump over the wire. Do this by guiding him through the poles with a big incentive. If he displays a tendency to want to jump the wire, prevent him from jumping by holding his collar (or leash or tab) and praising him continuously as he weaves. He will soon catch on. For dogs that continue to jump over the guides, use extra-high ones. Eventually you can transition to the lower ones.

Step #4 — Calling the Dog Through

One of the most important skills you can develop to improve your dog's weaving speed and independence is the ability to be called through the weave poles. Your dog will push his hardest when coming towards you. His footwork and head position will most likely be ideal. You will also be developing the dog's total weaving independence, since he will be weaving without any assistance from you. Although you will eventually want to be able to call him through regulation poles, it is best to start with short, offset poles.

A good time to start this training is when your dog is performing the offsets well off the left and the right with no guiding from your hand. Start with a short set of five or six poles.

Position two guides at the entrance to make it easy for your dog to start correctly. Also, since he will be very eager to reach you, it will be easy for him to skip the last pole. Therefore, to help him be successful, it is also a good idea to place another guide at the exit.

Place the dog in a sit-stay about one foot from the correct entrance to the poles. Alternatively, you may wish to have an assistant hold the dog in position and launch him when you give your command.

Position your right foot against the left side of the base of the weave poles at about the third pole. Hold a treat or toy in your right hand at the dog's nose level. Give your command to weave then begin backing up, luring the dog through the poles with the incentive.

Calling through the poles helps reinforce efficiency, footwork, speed, and weaving independence. Begin with a set of five or six weave poles and start about three poles back, as shown.

Use only a slight flick of your wrist rather than a dramatic zig-zag motion when luring the dog through the poles. Keep the incentive steady at the dog's nose level. Don't allow your hand to move up and down as your arm moves over the top of the poles. If this is difficult for you, use a dowel or clip stick to hold your incentive.

Praise and reward as he exits the last pole. Gradually increase the distance you lead out until you can call your dog through the entire set of offset poles.

Each time you are successful, start farther and farther away from the dog until you are calling him through the entire set of poles.

Step #5 — Developing Weave Pole Entry Skills

One of the most important skills you will need in agility is your dog's reliable entry to the weave poles. To be successful, your dog will need to be able to enter the poles at high speed from any angle, without assistance from you. In most styles of agility, missed weave pole entries are faulted as refusals, and they add many unwanted seconds to your agility runs.

Once your dog is reliable at being called through the offset poles from an ideal starting angle, you can begin making his entry angle more difficult. Use the same setup as you did to teach calling through, using guides for the entrance and exit.

Using wire guides, the dog learns to enter the weave poles confidently and independently at full speed and at any angle.

Place the dog about a foot to the right of an ideal starting angle. Go to the other end of the weave poles and call the dog through. If he needs extra help, you can start closer or you can add extra guides to make the entry more foolproof.

As the dog catches on, progress to more difficult angles, from both the left and right sides of the correct entry (Figure 6-2).

Next, start the dog farther and farther back from the poles, so he must enter correctly at a greater speed.

When he is doing well at entering the poles from various angles, you can work on teaching him to exit correctly without assistance from you. Instead of standing in the optimum position to call your dog through the poles, start slightly to the left or right. The guides will help your dog exit correctly. Gradually move your position to more extreme angles (Figure 6–3).

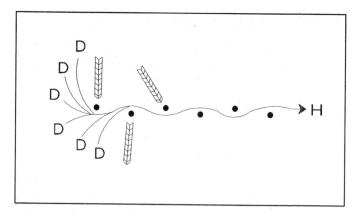

Figure 6-2: Teaching weave pole entry.

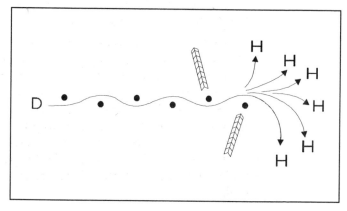

Figure 6-3: Teaching the dog to exit correctly.

Next, work on being able to move about freely while your dog is coming to you through the weave poles. You will need this skill to be able to cross in front of your dog on the weave poles. Start with slow, small movements then progress to faster, running movements.

Step #6 — Increasing Independence

In addition to calling through the weave poles, there are several other weave pole skills that will help your dog achieve solid weaving independence.

- **Parallel distance** — Gradually increase the distance you keep between you and your dog as you move alongside him. Eventually you want to be able to handle at a parallel distance of 20 - 30 feet away.

- **Getting ahead** — An important goal is to be able to run ahead of your dog as he is weaving, without fear that your movement will pull him out of the poles. Being able to get ahead of him gives you the flexibility to cross in front while he is weaving. It also allows you to get ahead to a position that may help indicate which obstacle is next.

- **Pulling away** — If a dog misses a weave pole, it is often the last pole. Sometimes this is because the dog has focused on the next obstacle. Other times it is because the handler has begun to pull away from the weave poles in an effort to move closer to the next obstacle. Work on being able to pull away from the poles as your dog is weaving. Use wire guides at first to help him succeed. Begin by moving away slowly and gradually. Progress to being able to run away suddenly with a sharp turn of your shoulders.

- **Sending through** — It is best to wait until the dog can call through quickly and reliably at a variety of angles before beginning training to send through. Since sequencing experience is useful when teaching your dog to send through the weave poles, that skill will be described in *Book 3: Advanced Skills Training.*

Step #7 — Developing Reliability

Of all the obstacles on the agility course, the weave poles require the most concentration on the part of your dog. Dogs can jump and run through the tunnels with only half their minds and attention on the obstacles, but weaving quickly and accurately requires complete concentration. One reason many dogs make weave-pole errors in competition is that they have not been trained to tune out all distractions and focus on their weaving.

Once your dog is performing solidly on the offset weave poles without help from you, you are ready to start teaching him to concentrate and avoid distractions. Start with a set of five or six offset weave poles. To help the dog be successful, you may want to position wire guides at the entrance and exit.

The distractions you use should be very mild at first. A person walking nearby or a distracting object placed on the ground several feet away can be enough to take the dog's concentration from his work. If he makes a mistake, at the precise moment of his infraction give a non-emotional verbal correction such as *Wrong!, Oops!,* or *Uh-oh!* This will help communicate to the dog exactly what was incorrect about what he just did, thus helping your training progress more quickly. Repeat immediately, making it easier for the dog to succeed. To do this, you might make the distracting person remain farther away or move the distracting object farther from view. Reward generously for concentrating on the task.

As your dog catches on to the game, gradually increase the level of distraction. Some dogs will be able to progress quite quickly to large distractions. More tentative dogs may need several weeks of gradually increasing distractions. Use your imagination to come up with interesting distractions. All is fair except things that might frighten or injure the dog. Suggestions include:

- **Squeaky toys** — Start by squeaking, then placing on the ground, then dropping on the ground, then stepping on, then throwing. Be careful not to let the dog reward himself for missing a weave pole.

- **Food** — Rattle a treat bag or sealed food container, drop it on the ground, toss it a short distance, have people hold treats at the dog's level while he is weaving, making sure to prevent the dog from rewarding himself if he leaves the poles to investigate.

- **Noise** — Place a radio or portable television near the poles. First play it quietly and then get progressively louder and closer to the dog's path.

- **People** — Have people walk, talk, sing, cheer, clap, and sit on the ground near the poles.

- **Mechanical toys** — Use children's toys such as battery-operated animals that make noises or music and jump or walk.

Most dogs grow to love the distraction game. Once they have caught on, they approach the poles with an attitude of "you can't fool me — it's a trick!" As a result, their speed, accuracy and confidence increase tremendously — even under the most distracting show conditions.

When your dog is performing well using a short set of offset poles with distractions, progress to a full set and then gradually remove the guides.

Step #8 — Transitioning to Regulation Poles

If you are training by yourself rather than in a group, you can gradually decrease the amount of the offset until the poles are in a straight line. Because it is not very practical to have dogs in class be at different stages in the amount of offset they re-quire, we transition directly from the offsets that are 1-1/2" from center to the straight-in-line-regulation poles. For the vast majority of dogs, this works very well, and class time is spent training rather than adjusting equipment.

While pioneering this method using one of my own dogs, something interesting occurred. I was in the training ring talk-ing to a friend while two of my goldens — eight-month-old Holly and her five-year-old mother Tracy — were roaming the ring foraging for treats dropped by students in the previous class. My friend asked to see Tracy work. I spotted a dog I thought was Tracy about 70 feet away and called her through a tunnel and through a set of 12 regulation poles, with a very difficult angle of entry. She flew through the tunnel, aced the weave pole entry and sailed through all of the poles with speed, efficient footwork, and absolute accuracy. To my surprise it was Holly and not Tracy (mother and daughter look alike)! Holly had never been through regulation poles, although she had mastered many skills on the offsets (we use only very flexible offsets so there is no wear and tear on a dog's developing body). I had been planning to transition her gradually from the 1-1/2" amount of offset until the poles were straight in line. Through my mistake in identity, I realized that it was possible to go directly from our offsets to the regulation poles.

It is important that your dog has mastered all of his skills on the offset poles before attempting the regulation poles. Start with a set of five or six regulation poles, with wire guides positioned at the entrance and exit. Approach the weave poles from the easiest angle for success. Watch the dog's footwork and head position. If they are not perfect, try using shorter poles and using your hand to lure the dog through. You can also try calling the dog through. This will often give the dog the forward drive and focus necessary to perform the poles to your high standards.

If your dog is still having trouble, return to the offset poles for more work, concentrating on calling the dog through.

> ***TRAINING TIP:*** *A good rule of thumb is, if you don't like something you're getting, stop! The more you drill weave poles with problems such as poor attitude, inefficient footwork and/or head position, or weaving only off the left, the harder it will be to convince your dog to perform otherwise. Old habits are hard to break. If at all possible, it's best to prevent unwanted behaviors from becoming habitual.*

Once the dog has successfully made the transition to the regulation poles, work through all of the reliability and independence skills you developed with the offsets. As your dog progresses, make sure you train with different numbered sets of poles. In competition you may encounter from five to twelve poles in a given set. If you always train with the same number, (such as 10), your dog may become a "pole counter" and exit early in a set of eleven or twelve. Make sure you also practice with both odd- and even-numbered sets of poles.

Don't consider the weave poles fully trained until you have taught your dog to weave quickly and accurately despite distracting conditions.

At a trial, you will encounter many different styles of weave poles. Some are stiff while some are very flexible. Bases can be flat or rounded, made out of metal or wood, or they may have no base at all, as in the case of stick-in-the-ground weave poles. To be prepared for any situation, practice on as many types of weave poles as possible. It is best, however, to delay exposure to very stiff metal poles until after the dog is fast and confident on flexible ones, and definitely until after the dog is physically mature.

Reliable performance on the contact obstacles is one of the biggest challenges in competitive agility, especially to handlers with very fast and/or enthusiastic dogs. (Photo: Critter Pictures)

7 Contact Obstacles

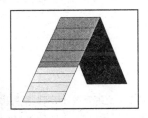

The contact obstacles include the **A-frame, dog walk** and **see-saw.** All are similar in that they contain ramps the dog must climb and descend. They also all contain **contact zones** — areas of contrasting color that the dog must touch with at least one part of one paw. There is a contact zone at the base of the upside and downside ramp of each contact obstacle. Reliable performance on the

contact obstacles is one of the biggest challenges in competitive agility, especially to handlers with very fast and/or enthusiastic dogs.

Getting your dog to reliably touch the contact zones in competition involves having a **contact handling strategy.** There are many strategies from which to choose. Unfortunately,

none of them is foolproof for all dogs at all times. In fact, a strategy that has been successful for months or even years may suddenly stop being effective. The handler must then retrain the current strategy or try another.

It's best to decide which contact-handling strategy you intend to use before you begin training any of the contact obstacles, because the lessons learned first tend to stick the best. Under stress or faced with uncertainty, dogs (and people, too!) tend to revert to their oldest habits.

Contact-Handling Strategies

Your contact-handling strategies will differ depending on whether you are controlling the downside or upside contact zones.

Downside Contact Zones

All agility handlers must have a plan for training and handling the downside contacts. Even the smallest or slowest of dogs can decide to leap off a contact obstacle before reaching the downside contact zone.

To choose a handling strategy, consider your preferences and your goals. Some methods require the handler to remain close to the dog while he performs the obstacle. Other methods allow the handler the flexibility of being in any position — from close to far from the dog.

METHODS THAT REQUIRE THE HANDLER TO REMAIN CLOSE TO THE DOG

- **Teaching the dog to match pace with the handler** so that if the handler takes smaller steps and slows down near the contact zone, the dog will do likewise. This method can be very successful. It is easy to train, reinforce, and correct. However, a major drawback of this strategy is that the handler needs to be alongside the dog — he cannot handle the zone at a distance or get ahead of the dog. Moreover, the dog's speed is limited by the speed of the handler.

- **The handler draws his hand down toward the ground as if luring the dog to the zone with a treat.** Like the method described above, this strategy is limiting in that the handler is an integral part of the process and must be close by to control the dog.

- **The handler runs to the end of the zone, faces the dog, squats down and issues a command to come.** When the dog reaches the contact zone, he may be asked to lie down. The handler then runs as quickly as possible to indicate the next obstacle. Although this technique has been used successfully to handle highly driven dogs, it has several disadvantages. The handler must be able to run faster than the dog to reach the end of the contact obstacle ahead of the dog. Furthermore, squatting in front of the dog often places the hander in a poor position to indicate the next sequence of obstacles. There is also a risk of being faulted for making physical contact with the dog, since the dog runs very close to the handler at the end of the zone.

METHODS THAT ALLOW DISTANCE HANDLING

Competitors at the more advanced levels have an advantage if they can handle the contact zones reliably at a distance. Doing so allows the dog to complete the obstacle at the dog's speed instead of being limited by the handler's. It also allows the handler to get ahead and more clearly indicate the next sequence when this would be advantageous. Distance handling on contacts can even be a necessity, such as when handlers are restricted from getting close to the zone by the placement of adjacent obstacles. It can also be required by the rules, as in a Gambler's course in which the dog must perform a series of obstacles away from the handler.

The following are some of the methods that provide the flexibility of handling zones either close by or at a distance:

- **The handler attempts to control the dog by issuing a command to wait when the dog touches the zone.** The problem with this strategy is that the dog may bail off the obstacle before he reaches the contact zone, never giving the handler the opportunity to command him to wait. To circumvent this problem, handlers may start issuing the *Wait!* command earlier, before the dog has reached the contact zone. If the dog obeys the command, the dog stops short of the zone. The handler is then left with the dilemma of encouraging the dog to walk one or two feet farther as the seconds tick away. On the other hand, if the dog doesn't wait but manages to hit the zone and is subsequently rewarded by the handler, the wait command has now weakened and changed. It no longer means *stay in position*. If you want *Wait!* to actually mean "wait" in other situations, such as the start line or on the pause table, your dog may not understand.

- **Teaching the dog to continue down the plank without slowing down or stopping, regardless of the handler's position.** Common commands for this strategy are *All the way!* or *Zone!* To be effective, you must describe the criteria for success. If you allow this command to mean *touch the contact zone and immediately exit the plank*, your dog will be rewarded for barely touching the zone. In competition, when the dog is more excited and distracted than he is in training, he will be likely to leave the plank before touching the zone.

  A better solution is to define success as touching the area between the first and second slat. This area is well below the start of the contact zone. If, in training, the dog touches the contact zone but does not touch the area between the first and second slat, he has not met your standards. The dog should not be rewarded.

  Training hoops can be an invaluable training aid to help ensure the dog performs correctly during training. Using hoops on a regular basis can help your dog develop the muscle memory to run smoothly down the ramp with his head lowered. Using an *All the way!* strategy works particularly well with small, short-strided dogs, or with slow to moderately paced dogs.

- **Teaching the dog to run quickly to a particular position on the downside contact and wait for further instructions.** The benefits to a command such as this are many.

  - The dog performs the contact quickly and accurately regardless of the handler's position or path.

  - The handler can get ahead of the dog when desired, even if the dog reaches the contact zone before he does.

  - It is easy to give a timely command for the next action before the dog exits the contact obstacle, since he is not permitted to leave until he is released.

  - It is easy to reward the dog at the exact position you want to reinforce.

One school of thought teaches a command many handlers call *Bottom!*, meaning *run quickly to the bottom of the contact, place your front feet on the ground and your back feet on the contact.* The dog must remain in position until he receives further instructions. This strategy works quite well for many handlers. *Bottom!* is initially trained using a target (such as a treat placed on a margarine container lid) positioned on the ground near the base of the contact zone. Eventually the target is weaned away, using progressively smaller and less visible targets.

An advantage to using *Bottom!* Is that the dog has a very concrete position to assume. The texture of the ground is different from that of the plank, which makes it relatively easy for the dog to find the position you desire. A disadvantage is that it can cause strain to the dog's back while performing the A-frame. It can also cause back strain for very small dogs on the see-saw. Moreover, using a *Bottom!* strategy does nothing to prevent fly-offs (course penalties in which the dog leaves the see-saw plank before it touches the ground).

In our classes we currently teach a similar command called *Spot!* that means *run quickly to the last slat (front feet above the last slat, or equivalent position for slatless contact obstacles) and wait for further instructions.* The dog must remain in place until released with a release word, a *Come!* command, or the command for the next obstacle. One of the benefits of *Spot!* over *Bottom!* is that it can be slightly more practical for use in class. During both training and maintenance stages of the spot method, food is placed on the obstacle rather than the ground. With the bottom method, students tend to get in a hurry and neglect to put out their targets. They are likely to instead place the food directly on the ground which encourages the unwanted behavior of sniffing around and searching for food.

Using the *Spot!* command, once the behavior is trained, food can be placed on the underside of the slat. The resulting benefit is that the dog is never sure if he will find a treat on the contact until he has touched the zone. Because no visible targets are used, the training setup appears identical to the one the dog will encounter in the ring. For this reason, the *Spot!* command is particularly successful for independent dogs who need to think there may be a reward available (as opposed to a dog who works the contact because that is his job). This method also tends to work well with highly driven dogs of every size, from Border Collies to Jack Russell Terriers. It is easier for many of these dogs to run full-speed then stop, then run full-speed again, than to slow down while running.

Another benefit to using *Spot!* is that handlers can encourage a speedy see-saw performance without fear of fly-offs, since the dog is trained to run quickly to the end of the plank and remain there until released. The result is a lightning-fast see-saw performance, which provides a competitive edge.

In a nutshell, the *Spot!* command is trained as follows: First, food is placed on the visible side of the last slat every time the dog performs the contact obstacle. Then it is placed on the underside of the slat. Next, it is sometimes placed on the underside and sometimes placed on the slat after the dog has run to the last slat and is waiting. Eventually, the food is only placed on the underside of the slat on rare occasions.

Once the dog has begun sequencing, he runs to the spot and looks to the handler. The handler commands the next obstacle (from among a choice of obstacles), the dog complies and is given a jackpot reward. The dog learns to run quickly to the spot to earn the opportunity to complete one or more obstacles for the possibility of a jackpot reward. By transferring the timing of your reward to an obstacle that comes after the contact obstacle, you avoid the problem of the dog realizing that there will be no food on the contacts at a real trial. By the time the dog would normally expect a reward, he is already in the midst of a fast-paced sequence.

The procedures in this chapter for training each of the contact obstacles incorporate *Spot!* as a downside contact handling strategy. You may easily substitute your choice of strategies if you prefer another.

Using the Spot! *command, the dog runs quickly to the last slat and looks at the handler for direction to the next obstacle.*

Upside Contact Zones

Dogs can earn faults for missing upside contacts for two reasons: either the dog does not ascend the ramp squarely, or the dog ascends squarely but takes too large a stride, leaping over the zone when entering the plank. Faults earned for the first reason — sloppy plank approaches — are easy to prevent. In your agility training, **always** require the dog to enter the plank squarely. If he does not, give a well-timed verbal correction, pick him up off the obstacle, and help to re-enter the plank properly. Follow with praise and a reward. Using wire guides all or most of the time is a good way to make proper plank entry a habit. With well-trained, reliable plank approaches, most handlers will not have to worry about upside contacts.

The second cause affects only large, long-legged dogs. If their approach stride is longer than the contact zone, you will have to train the dog to take a smaller stride when ascending the plank, or to time his stride so as to reliably touch the zone. There are several methods to accomplish this.

- **Teach the dog to slow down and match the handler's pace** using a command such as *Easy!* or *Heel!*. One drawback is that the handler has to be with the dog, and the dog's speed is limited by that of his handler. Another disadvantage is that this method reduces the dog's speed when approaching contacts, adding extra time to your run.

  In a similar fashion, some handlers call their dogs to *Come!* before the dog approaches the contact, then help their dogs to carefully handle the approach. Others command their dogs to *Lie Down!*, hoping that the dog will only think about lying down, thereby slowing the dog's approach. These techniques can work — but be careful. If your dog actually does lie down in front of the contact obstacle you may earn a refusal fault. Likewise, if you pull your dog off his approach to the contact obstacle at the last minute, you may also incur a penalty for a *handler-induced* refusal.

- **Use training hoops** on a regular basis in your training from the very start so that the dog develops a habit of ducking his head and touching the zone when ascending the ramp. For best results, position the hoop approximately even with the area you want the dog to touch. This method generally takes months of patterning. If you are retraining a dog who has been allowed to miss upsides in the past, the training will take even longer.

- **Place a treat on the upside,** high enough so that the dog must board the ramp to get it, but low enough so that the dog will not take a leaping stride, lest he bypass the treat. Like the use of training hoops, this method requires months of patterning.

- **Reward the dog for touching a target** or specific area of the contact zone on the upside ramp. It can be difficult to isolate and reward correct performance, since split-second timing is required. (A clicker or other conditioned reinforcer can be useful with this method.) It can also be difficult to give a timely verbal correction. As a result, your dog may have difficulty discovering what you want and what you do not want.

In your early on-leash training of the contact obstacles, you will not be able to use upside hoops. However, you can ensure that your highly driven dog touches the upsides by applying slight backward pressure to the leash as he approaches the obstacle.

Once you are working off-leash, use hoops on a regular basis to help a long-legged dog develop the muscle memory to touch the upside contacts.

Using upside hoops on a continuous basis, the dog acquires the "muscle memory" to lower his head and touch the zone when approaching the contact obstacles. Shown is a stick-in-the-ground hoop.

Base-mounted hoops are useful alternatives to in-ground hoops, but they can be difficult to place under ramps.

Common Contact Training Mistakes

Mistakes made during your training sessions can contribute to poor performance on the contact obstacles. A few common training mistakes include:

- **Issuing multiple commands** — Repeating your *Spot!* command (or whatever your zone command may be) teaches your dog to rely on you to tell him when he has complied. Consider this example: Your dog stops short of the contact zone so you repeat your *Spot!* command. He inches down another slat and you again repeat your command. After four commands and ten seconds the dog has touched the contact zone. Congratulations! You have just taught your dog to waste countless seconds inching down the ramp to the contact zone one slat at a time. To avoid this problem, in training give only one *Spot!* command (which means *run quickly to the last slat and await further instructions*). If the dog stops short of the last slat, point out the desired location — without repeating your command. Tell him *Good Spot!* the moment his feet reach the desired location, then release. Next time make it easy for the dog to be successful by showing the dog a treat at the last slat.

- **Giving commands that have no specific or trained meaning** — Are you guilty of using contact-handling commands that you have never systematically trained? Worse yet — do you use commands you cannot clearly define? If so, how can you expect your dog to understand what you want and be successful?

- **Changing the meaning of your commands throughout your training** — If your *Zone!* command means *place a foot between slats 1 and 2 or lower* and you allow the dog to barely hit the contact zone in training, you have changed the meaning of your command. If you allow this to continue, your dog's response is likely to become weaker and weaker, until he is missing the zones completely.

- **Allowing zone infractions to go uncorrected in practice** — Many handlers are tempted to overlook missed contact zones during training, especially when practicing a course. Often the rationale for this is that the handler wants to see what his time would have been. Don't fall into this trap! What you will have accomplished is to teach your dog that it is not necessary to touch the contact zones while running a course.

- **Never training under distracting or exciting conditions** — If you have never asked your dog to work with you in practice under distracting conditions, how can you expect him to do so at an agility trial? Once your dog has learned his contact zone skills in a distraction-free environment, you cannot consider those skills truly trained until you deliberately add distractions and work through them.

Common Contact Handling Mistakes

You can further improve your dog's reliability on the contact zones by avoiding some common handling mistakes.

- **Crowding contact zones** — Some handlers train at a comfortable distance during training, but crowd their dogs (perhaps out of worry or panic) on the zones at a trial. Often however, this invades the dog's buffer zone and pushes him off the contact.

  Another consequence of crowding contacts in the competition ring is that it forces the judge to run close behind you, which may distract or spook your dog. Handling at a moderate distance from the contacts keeps the judge farther away from you and your dog.

- **Frantic tone of voice** — In the competition ring, it's common for handlers' voices to sound more frantic than during training. This is usually counterproductive. When the handler sounds frantic, the dog is likely to become even more excited, and is more likely to miss a zone. A frantic voice also makes the handler appear less in control of the situation, which can result in the dog taking more control or engaging in his own activities.

- **Lifting head up to see next obstacle** — If a handler is focused on the contact zone and suddenly looks up to find the next obstacle, his motion may cause his dog to leave the plank prematurely.

A-Frame

PICTURE OF PERFECT PERFORMANCE

The dog scales the A-frame quickly and without hesitation, touching the upside contact zone. He scrambles over the top and immediately runs to the bottom, touching the downside contact.

General Rules

The dog must ascend the A-frame ramp, touching the upside contact zone. (In some styles of agility, failure to touch the upside contact of the A-frame is not faulted.) He must then traverse the apex and descend the opposite side, touching the downside contact before he exits.

Commands

Common commands include *A-frame!*, *Scramble!*, *Frame!*, *Wall!*, and *Climb!*. Because the obstacle has a unique appearance, the command you choose should be one that is unique to the A-frame.

Step #1 — Introduction to the Lowered A-Frame

You will need an assistant to teach your dog the A-frame. The assistant's job will be to place a treat (soft, sticky treats work best) on the last slat of the down ramp for each repetition before the dog approaches the obstacle. He will also serve as a spotter to prevent the dog from jumping or falling off the obstacle on the side opposite the handler. While spotting, the assistant should also entice the dog up the ramp.

> **TRAINING TIP:** *The goal is for your dog to run at full speed to the end of the contact without waiting for his handler. To help ensure that this happens, be sure you or your assistant places food treats on the contact before your dog begins his ascent. If you become lazy and put down the treat with your hand as the dog descends, he will learn to hang back and wait for you, since there will be no treat in place until you catch up with him.*

Start with an A-frame adjusted to a height of four feet or lower. With your dog on leash, start about 15 feet from the A-frame. Position your dog to have a straight path up the A-frame, and extend your arm so that your path will be outside of the edge of the obstacle, with your outside shoulder turned slightly inward.

Focus your dog's attention ahead toward the A-frame. Give your command, then begin moving toward the obstacle. As he crosses the apex, give your *Spot!* command. Help point out the spot, without repeating your command. If you notice the dog beginning to descend the ramp sideways, prevent him from doing so by placing a hand or finger by his loin.

At the moment his front feet reach the spot, say *Good spot!*, *Wait!* and place another treat on the slat. The reason to put the treat on the slat rather than let the dog eat it from your hand is your dog may soon begin to cut out the middleman and exit the contact early to save you the trouble of coming to the slat. If the treat is always delivered to the slat, the dog will be perfectly satisfied to wait there for as long as you like.

Give your Spot! *command the moment the dog begins his descent.*

After delivering the treat to the slat, stand upright immediately. Don't crowd the dog on the contact zone. Your dog should be looking at you now, wondering if you are going to put yet another goodie on the slat. Release with a *Come!* command straight off the plank. Work both off the right as well as off the left.

> **TRAINING TIP:** *Do not allow the dog to linger on the spot sucking every last bit of treat from the slat. The* Spot! *command is a limited-time offer. When you command the dog to* Come!, *expect an immediate response. If the dog does not comply immediately, do not repeat your command! Instead, give a pop and release (not a drag!) with the leash or tab, followed by immediate praise.*

DEALING WITH A RELUCTANT DOG

Do your best to avoid dragging a reluctant dog up the A-frame. Instead, try one or more of the following:

- Lower the height of the A-frame to make it easier to succeed.

- Use a better or bigger incentive, or start with a hungrier dog.

- Have an assistant restrain the dog while exciting him with phrases like *"On your mark!"* or *"Are you ready?"* Many dogs will pull forward against the restraint. When released, the added impulsion may help the dog up the A-frame.

- Check the dog's weight. An overweight dog can have a difficult time climbing even a lowered A-frame.

- Check the dog's nails. Dogs with nails that are too long may find it painful to climb the A-frame or any of the other contact obstacles.

Step #2 — Increasing the Height

When the dog is comfortably performing the A-frame on his own power and is running directly to the last slat and waiting, without stopping short, you can begin to raise the height about four to six inches. Continue to progress until the A-frame is at competition height. This height will vary depending on the style of agility in which you will be competing.

Step #3 — Reinforcing the Wait

As the dog descends the ramp and reaches the last slat, continue to take a step or two. If the dog waits, return to the dog and praise and reward him on the slat for waiting. If he doesn't wait, give an immediate verbal correction such as *Uh-oh!*, pick up the dog and place him back in position. Take a smaller or slower step the next time to help him be successful. Progress to being able to run away from the A-frame at full speed, while the dog remains steady on the plank. Return to the plank to reward success.

> **TRAINING TIP:** *Be careful not to habitually couple your dog's release with the start of a concurrent body motion. You may inadvertently make your sudden movement signify a release from the contact for your dog.*

Step #4 — Gradually Eliminating Food on the Slat

Once the dog is running directly to the food on the last slat every time without hesitation and without help from you or your assistant, you can begin to wean the dog off the food. Start by showing the dog you are putting a treat on the slat. When he is not looking, move it to the underside of the slat so that he will not see it until he is in the contact zone.

Set up for an approach to the A-frame. Give your obstacle command and tell the dog *Spot!*, as before, when he crosses the apex. The dog should go straight to the last slat. If he stops short, point out the desired position but do not repeat your command. As a last resort, use verbal encouragement but do not repeat the *Spot!* command. As soon as the dog's front feet touch the last slat tell him *Good spot!*, *Wait!*, and show him the treat on the underside if he hasn't already found it. When he has eaten it, place another goodie immediately on the slat. Stand upright — don't hover. Tell him *Good wait!* and place yet another small treat on the slat. Release with a *Come!* command and enforce, if necessary. At this point, alternate between sometimes having a treat on the visible side of the slat and sometimes having it on the underside.

When he is reliably running to the last slat regardless of whether the treat is visible or not, alternate between sometimes having the treat on the underside and sometimes having no treat at all. When there is no treat, be sure to praise immediately with *Good spot!* and place a treat on the slat with your signaling hand (the hand closest to the dog).

You want the *Spot!* command to work exactly the same regardless of your position in relation to the dog. To achieve this, make sure you vary your body position on successive attempts. Sometimes run ahead of the dog. Sometimes hang back or remain stationary. Sometimes handle close to the dog. Other times handle at a distance.

Gradually decrease the frequency with which you place food on the underside of the slat, until you only do so only on rare occasions. When there is no food, sometimes you will deliver a treat to the slat, other times you will give only praise.

> **TRAINING TIP:** *Never allow the dog to release himself on your praise! You want to be able to tell the dog he is doing a good job without ending the exercise.*

Eventually your dog will be running to the spot immediately and looking at you with rapt attention. Once you have begun sequencing, you can give an obstacle command when the dog has reached the spot. Follow with a jackpot reward. Repeat, varying the obstacle that follows the contact, so that the dog does not anticipate which obstacle you will send him to. Progress to giving the jackpot after one, two, or three obstacles after the contact.

It will now be very easy to make the transition to a ring situation in which no food will be on the slat. Running quickly to the spot will earn your dog an opportunity to complete one or more subsequent obstacles for a jackpot. In competition, the dog will be in the midst of a fast-moving sequence of obstacles, and will not have time to wonder why he has not yet received a cookie!

Step #4 — Adding Distance and Angles

Once the dog is very confident performing the A-frame at full height without assistance, it is time to begin working at a distance.

CALLING

Leave the dog on a stay or have someone hold him about 15 feet in front of the A-frame. Go to the opposite side of the obstacle to a place where the dog can still see you. Give your command and signal for the A-frame. Gradually increase the angle and distance at which you set him up to approach the obstacle. It may be helpful to position wire guides to help him line himself up correctly for the approach.

SENDING

Show the dog a treat placed on the last slat but don't allow him to have it. Take the dog to the ascending side of the obstacle and line him up for a straight approach. Give your command and signal and begin moving toward the obstacle. Instead of continuing to the downside with the dog, hang back and go only part way. (Don't forget to give an enthusiastic *Spot!* command when the dog has reached the apex.) Come to a gliding halt rather than an abrupt stop. If necessary, have an assistant point out the treat on the slat. Do not repeat your command. Progress to being able to hang back more and more until the dog performs the entire obstacle correctly without your moving forward.

Gradually increase the angle and distance at which you position the dog to approach the obstacle. It may be helpful to use wire guides to help the dog align himself correctly for the approach and descent.

PARALLEL DISTANCE

Gradually increase the parallel distance between you and your dog as you move alongside him while he performs the obstacle. Progress to a parallel distance of 30 feet between you and the obstacle. Use wire guides or hoops to ensure that the dog enters and exits the ramps squarely.

Teach your dog to align himself for the approach to the A-frame using wire guides.

Dog Walk

PICTURE OF PERFECT PERFORMANCE

The dog approaches the dog walk squarely, quickly, and without hesitation, touching the upside contact zone. He races across the top plank and immediately runs to the bottom, cleanly touching the downside contact.

General Rules

The dog must ascend the dog walk ramp, touching the upside contact zone. He must then continue to the descending ramp and touch the downside contact before he exits.

Commands

Common commands include *Dog walk!*, *Plank!*, *Walk it!*, and *Ramp!*. Because of its unique sight picture, choose a command that is unique to the dog walk.

Step #1 — Introduction to Plank Walking

Before attempting the actual dog walk it is helpful to introduce the dog to walking on a simple plank. To create this setup, use two sturdy storage crates and one of the planks from your see-saw or dog walk. The crates will lift the plank about a foot off the ground.

For a small dog you may want to begin by placing the dog at the beginning of the plank. Larger dogs can easily mount the plank on their own. It is not important what command you use for the plank because you will only be using it a few times. Feel free to use the command you have chosen for the dog walk or use encouragement only with no command.

Step #2 — Introduction to the Dog Walk

When the dog is walking the plank with speed and confidence, you may progress to the dog walk. It's best to start with a lowered dog walk if one is available.

You will need an assistant to help you as described for the A-frame. Start with your dog on a leash or a tab. Have your assistant show your dog a treat on the last slat. Pick the dog up and place him a foot or so from the last slat on the down ramp. Command *Spot!* and help point out the treat. Make sure that you and the assistant do not let the dog jump or fall off the ramp. When he reaches the treat, command *Good spot! Wait!*, and then place small bits of food on the slat, while saying *Good wait!* as described for the A-frame. Release with a *Come!* command and enforce, if necessary.

As the dog gains confidence, place the dog higher and higher on the down ramp to start. This is called **backchaining**. If your dog is too heavy for you and your assistant to lift, you may have to skip the backchaining and begin at the upside ramp. Alternatively, you could start with a plank with one end resting securely on a pause table.

When you have progressed to beginning at the up ramp of the dog walk, give your command for the obstacle before you start moving toward it. Always command *Spot!* when the dog begins his descent.

For dogs that have difficulty placing their back feet on the plank, use wire guides or broad jump boards placed on their sides on both sides of the plank.

DEALING WITH THE KAMIKAZE DOG

Some dogs may become so excited or frantic that they will try to race across the plank recklessly, with no regard to their personal safety. With these dogs it is essential to have two ever-vigilant spotters. The dog needs to learn how to place his feet to negotiate the dog walk safely. It may be helpful to place a treat on every slat or every other slat to slow the dog down until he is more experienced. You could also try using a non-restrictive harness that is controlled from above the dog's back.

Step #2 — Increasing the Height

When the dog is comfortably performing the dog walk on his own power and is running directly to the last slat and waiting, without stopping short, you can begin to raise the height about four to six inches at a time. Continue to progress until the dog walk is at competition height.

Step #3 — Reinforcing the Wait

Follow the steps described for the A-frame.

Step #4 — Gradually Eliminating Food on the Slat

Follow the steps described for the A-frame.

Step #5 — Calling, Sending, and Adding Distance and Angles

Follow the steps described for the A-frame. Use wire guides to help teach your dog to align himself for the entrance and exit.

Use wire guides to train your dog to enter and exit the dog walk ramps squarely.

See-Saw

PICTURE OF PERFECT PERFORMANCE

The dog swiftly approaches the see-saw without hesitation and cleanly touches the upside contact zone. He moves swiftly to the end of the plank controlling the board all along, though not hesitating at the board's pivot point. The dog then touches the downside contact zone and exits the board immediately as it touches the ground.

General Rules

The dog must ascend the see-saw ramp, touching the upside contact zone. He then must control the plank as it tilts downward and touch the downside contact zone. The board must touch the ground before the dog exits the plank. Failure to touch one or both of the contact zones is faulted. Leaving the plank before it touches the ground or running across the plank in an uncontrolled fashion is faulted as a **fly-off**.

Commands

Common commands include *See-saw!* and *Teeter!* Do not use the same command you use for the dog walk or A-frame. The see-saw has a unique appearance and performance, so the dog should be able to recognize the obstacle by its verbal command alone.

Step #1 — Introduction to the Lowered See-Saw

It is a good idea to introduce the see-saw only after your dog is comfortable performing the dog walk. As with all of the contact obstacles, you will need an assistant to teach your dog the see-saw. If at all possible, start with a see-saw that is substantially lower than regulation height. This will give your dog a better chance for a confident and successful start.

Before each repetition, place a treat at the last slat of the see-saw. Because the plank will be moving, sticky treats work best. If you are using a see-saw that does not have slats, place a sticky treat near the end of the contact zone, roughly where you would place it if the plank contained slats.

Start with your dog on leash at your left side, in a direct line with and about eight feet from the entrance to the see-saw. Hold the dog's leash close to the collar with your right hand. If you have a large dog, you may want to hold the dog's collar itself for the best control. Make sure all excess leash is gathered and held in your right hand so that it does not interfere with your dog's movement. Your left hand should remain available to help steady the dog as necessary as he traverses the plank.

Focus the dog's attention ahead to the see-saw. Your assistant can help by calling the dog's name and showing him a toy or a treat in his hand above the plank. Give your command for the see-saw and begin moving toward the plank. Have your assistant lure the dog up the plank using the incentive, while helping control the plank with his other hand.

When the dog takes at least a full step past the point on the plank where it begins to move, quietly tell him to wait, and hold him steady in position. (Be careful not to stop your dog too soon or put too much emphasis on waiting, or you will teach your dog to waste countless seconds on the see-saw.) If the dog is resistant to waiting, have the assistant hold a treat in his hand at the waiting point and allow him to nibble on it. While the dog is eating, have your assistant slowly lower the plank to the ground. Once the board has stopped moving, give your *Spot!* command and allow the dog to continue forward to the last slat (or its equivalent on non-slatted see-saws).

TRAINING TIP: *Watch the dog's head as he negotiates the plank. If he looks to the side rather than ahead, it may be a sign that he is thinking about jumping off the board. Prevent this from happening by being observant. At the first sign of the dog looking to the side, re-focus his attention forward with a toy or treat.*

As the dog gains confidence, allow the plank to move faster and hit the ground with greater impact. It may help to cushion the impact with foam rubber or other shock-absorbing material, and then gradually eliminate it. As soon as the dog learns how to control the plank, eliminate the command to *Wait!* and instead tell the dog to *Spot!* once all four feet are on the see-saw plank.

Be sure to work off the right as well as off the left.

DEALING WITH THE RELUCTANT DOG

Avoid pulling and dragging the dog that appears reluctant. This will usually cause him to become even more hesitant. Instead, start with a hungrier dog and a better incentive. (Yes, we've even used pizza and cheeseburgers!) Once the dog learns there is nothing to fear, you will be able to discontinue these special incentives. Don't despair. With time and patience, every dog learns to master the see-saw. As an alternative, you might try putting a bit of food on each slat (every foot or so for non-slatted see-saws).

For dogs that have difficulty placing their back feet on the plank, use wire guides or broad jump boards placed on their sides on both sides of the plank.

Step #2 — Raising the Height

When the dog is quickly and happily performing the lowered see-saw and is controlling the board on his own, you may begin raising the height. Each time you raise the board, begin by helping control the plank and preventing it from slamming to the ground. Progress to allowing the dog to totally control the plank.

Step #3 — Reinforcing the Wait

Follow the steps described for the A-frame.

Step #4 — Gradually Eliminating Food on the Slat

Follow the steps described for the A-frame, using wire guides or hoops to help teach your dog to align himself for the entrance and exit.

Step #5 — Adding Distance and Angles

Follow the steps described for the A-frame.

Step #6 —Training for a Variety of See-saw Styles

In Novice-level competition, many dogs have problems with the see-saw. Commonly, the dog gets on the see-saw once then refuses to do so again. It can come as a huge surprise to you when your dog is performing flawlessly on your see-saw at home, but displays fear and reluctance at a trial.

See-saws can vary from one another in many ways. Some have slats and some do not. Appearances can also vary slightly. Most problems, however, come from variations in noise-level and the pivot point of the see-saw.

Some metal see-saws can be very noisy. When the trial is held on a firm surface, the noise is even more pronounced. If you can't gain access to a noisy, metal see-saw, place a metal cookie sheet under the downside plank to simulate the noise. You can also cheer while banging a metal saucepan with a spoon as the dog is performing the see-saw to acclimate him an even noisier, yet festive atmosphere.

The see-saws you encounter in competition will be weighted in different ways. Some are heavily weighted toward the up-side, so that the board tips early. Some are heavily weighted at the downside so the dog needs to travel farther on the plank before it tips. If your dog has not had experience performing see-saws with varying pivot points, he is likely to jump off the see-saw in the competition ring, when the board tips earlier or later than expected.

To train for this, you do not need to purchase several different see-saws. Instead, you can attach weights in a temporary fashion at varying points along your see-saw plank. Flat weights of the 1-1/2- to 2-pound variety work well. You can tape them securely to the plank with duct tape. When your dog becomes confident with the new pivot point, change it again until you feel confident he can handle any situation.

Maintaining Contact Performance

Once your dog is performing each of the contact obstacles with confidence, speed, and accuracy, it is time to proof him for reliability under a variety of conditions.

In competition, your dog will be required to run at full speed in a very exciting atmosphere. To be successful, your dog will need to ignore all distractions, control his excitement, and perform the contact obstacles accurately regardless of his environment. Therefore, it is essential that your training program include proofing for reliability on the contact obstacles.

To simulate the excitement of competition and to make sure you dog understands his job, have one or more friends help provide a distracting atmosphere as your dog performs each of the contact obstacles. Start with mild distractions and gradually progress to stronger ones. Distractions can include food, toys, noise, and people moving near the dog. All is fair except anything that might frighten or injure the dog. Eventually, your dog should perform the contacts with speed, focus, and accuracy while your friends are cheering, clapping, throwing balls, toys, and dropping or throwing containers of food.

During your proofing sessions on contacts, your dog may make a mistake in one of two ways:

- He may stop prematurely on the way to the spot position.

- He may release himself from the contact to investigate the distraction.

Neither of these situations conforms to your picture of perfect performance, therefore, you should enforce a zero-tolerance policy on infractions of this type. With either mistake, at the precise moment of his infraction, give a non-emotional verbal correction such as *Wrong!*, *Oops!*, or *Uh-oh!* This will help communicate to the dog exactly what was incorrect about what he just did, thus helping your training progress more quickly.

If your dog stops short of the last slat...

Don't repeat your *Spot!* command. This will only teach him to make successive approximations and to rely on you for extra commands. Instead, point out the correct position with the hand closest to the dog (your signaling hand) and place a treat at the last slat, if there is not already one there. Use verbal encouragement, if necessary, but do not repeat your *Spot!* command. When he reaches the position, tell him *Good spot!*, and pet him but don't let him eat the treat. Tell him to *Come!*, (and enforce, if necessary). Move the treat to the underside of the slat, while your dog watches and try again immediately. This time, back off slightly on the level of distraction you are using. You want the dog to be correct. If he does not achieve success on successive attempts he may decide the game is no longer fun for him and he will stop trying to get it right.

> **TRAINING TIP:** *If your dog stops short of the last slat don't drag him to the spot. This only triggers opposition reflex, where the dog puts on the breaks to resist your dragging. You will have better success if you work to find ways to entice the dog to run quickly to the spot on his own power.*

If your dog is successful on your next attempt; that is, he runs immediately to the last slat on one command despite distractions; place an extra-special reward on the slat once he arrives there and let him know he is wonderful. If you have a dog that has a low tolerance for repetition, release with a *Come!* command and quit this exercise for today. Otherwise, you may want to try increasing the level of distraction slightly on your next attempt.

If your dog releases himself without your permission...

Give your verbal correction at the moment of the infraction and prevent the dog from rewarding himself with any of your distractions, such toys or food. Pick him up, place him in position, and tell him *Good spot!* Give him praise and petting but no food reward. Release him from the contact and show him a reward on the underside of the slat but do not let him eat it. On the next attempt, back off slightly on the level of the distraction. You want the dog to be successful. Give a jackpot reward for getting it right, then either quit for the day or try again, with a slightly stronger distraction.

MAINTAINING CONTACT RELIABILITY

Reliable contacts are not something that you train once and will continue to have forever after. In your quest to turn in blue-ribbon performances you will be pushing your dog to run at his highest possible speed. To achieve the fastest time in competition, you will often release your dog the moment he has touched the contact zone, rather than making him continue to the bottom slat before release. Over time, your dog may begin anticipating the release to help you in your quest for the fastest time. Unfortunately, he may begin to release himself earlier and earlier, incurring faults for missed contacts in the process.

Accurate contact performance requires regular maintenance. Like your car, house, or anything else, things that are not maintained have a tendency to weaken. In dog training, behaviors that are not reinforced and strengthened lose precision. Downs on the table become slower, stays becomes less solid, and contacts become less reliable. To maintain fast and accurate performance on the contact obstacles, the most successful agility trainers incorporate proofing exercises in their training sessions throughout their dogs' agility careers.

_8_ Jumps and the Tire Jump

Jumps

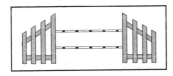

On an agility course you will encounter an enormous variety of jumps that can take on many appearances. The majority of jumps on a course are **single jumps.** These are jumps that require the dog to clear a single bar or board at a given height — there is no additional challenge of a depth requirement.

Jumps that use boards rather than bars are called **panel jumps.** Panel jumps offer the additional challenge of resembling a solid wall that the dog cannot see through.

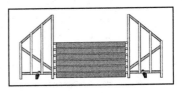

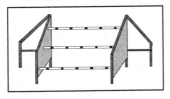

An agility course may also contain **spread jumps.** These are jumps that require the dog to jump several bars at a given width span, while also clearing a given height. Common spread jumps include the double-bar jump and the triple-bar jump.

On both single and spread jumps, the bars or boards are supported by narrow or wide uprights. Jumps with wide uprights (wings) are called **winged jumps;** jumps with narrow uprights are called **non-winged** or **wingless** jumps. Most courses contain a mixture of winged and wingless jumps (Figure 8-1). Each has its own advantages and disadvantages.

Winged jumps can be a challenge for novice dogs, since the wings prevent the handler from running closely alongside the dog. What's more, wings can be decorated in any number of ways. The unusual appearance of some elaborately decorated jump wings can challenge the novice dog, who may be surprised, curious, or even frightened by the jumps.

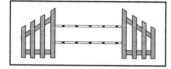 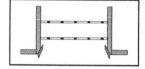

Figure 8-1: Winged and wingless single jumps.

Wingless jumps, on the other hand, can be more difficult for the dog to see than winged jumps. Since there is little substance to them, wingless jumps can easily blend in with the background in the agility ring. Thus, dogs traveling at high speeds or making sharp turns may be more likely to bypass wingless jumps in competition.

Smart Jumping

Since competition agility courses are never revealed before the day of the trial and are never the same twice, your dog's performance cannot be patterned. The spacing between obstacles, the ground footing, and the type and number of turns required are always varied and unpredictable. To be truly competitive, your dog must learn to be a smart jumper — adjusting his stride, style, and take-off point to most efficiently address the ring conditions and course requirements.

The picture of perfect performance is the same for all types of jumps.

Jump wings can be decorated in almost any way imaginable. (Top photo: Pat Vandecapelle)

PICTURE OF PERFECT PERFORMANCE

The dog soars over the jump without stutter-stepping or hesitation, from a variety of angles, without displacing a bar or board. The dog leaves the ground at an optimum distance from the jump, automatically adjusting for obstacle spacing and course layout. He jumps efficiently without wasting effort, clearing each bar or board cleanly but without excess clearance, regardless of the height of the jump.

General Rules

The dog must clear the jump without displacing a bar or board, which is faulted. Running under a bar or board is scored as a refusal.

Commands

Common commands for the jumps include *Over!, Jump!,* and *Hup!* An advantage of choosing *Jump!* or *Hup!* is that these commands are only one syllable in length, so they are faster to say. When running a very fast dog, this can be an advantage. A disadvantage is that these words both sound similar to the command *Come!,* which is a command that is commonly used to turn the dog toward the handler when sequencing.

Step #1 — Recalls

Start with a wingless bar jump with the bar set at the dog's elbow height or lower. (You can repeat the process later using a wingless panel jump.) For very small or young dogs, bars placed on the ground between the two jump uprights may be appropriate.

Attach your dog to a six-foot nylon or leather lead and place him in a sit-stay or have an assistant hold him about four feet in front of the jump. Step over the bar to the other side of the jump, holding the leash in your hand. With your free hand, tap the bar, give your command to jump (do not use your *Come!* command), and begin to back up. Praise and reward.

Most dogs will happily jump the hurdle to reach the handler. For those that show reluctance, squeak a toy or shake a food container to get the dog's attention, then throw the object a short distance ahead when the dog clears the jump.

> **TRAINING TIP**: *When having an assistant hold your dog in position, don't put the dog in a sit or tell him to stay. If he breaks, you will be forced to return to your dog and enforce your command. This takes time away from your agility training and makes it less fun for your dog. Worse yet, if you don't go back and enforce the command, you have just taught your dog that your* stay *command is optional.*

If the dog knocks a bar during this learning stage, say nothing if he is emotionally sensitive. If he is not, give a non-emotional verbal correction such as *Uh-oh!* as the bar is falling. In either situation, repeat the obstacle and reward lavishly for keeping the bar up. If the dog knocks the bar a second time, lower the jump height to help him be successful.

WHY LEAVE YOUR DOG IN A SIT BEFORE A JUMP?

When starting a training exercise or when running at trials, you are free to leave your dog in any position you desire: sit, down, or stand. It's a good idea, however, to leave your dog in a sit. There are several reasons for this.

If you leave your dog in a stand and he breaks his stay, he will be moving forward from the moment he breaks. If he breaks a sit, he will probably stand first. Although not ideal, this situation is not usually disastrous.

Even more important, your dog is more likely to take off smoothly and clear the first jump of a sequence if left in a sit. This is especially true when the space from the dog's starting position to the jump is limited. From a sitting position, the dog can immediately move into a canter to the jump take-off point. The other positions require the dog to take a step or two to establish the canter before beginning the jump.

JUMPING WITH YOUNG DOGS AND PUPPIES

Be extremely cautious when jumping puppies and adolescent dogs. Their growing bodies are very fragile. Even a minor injury could cause permanent damage. Make sure all jumps are set at the dog's elbow height or lower, and refrain from excessive repetitions or drilling. Your campaign to work toward full-height jumping can begin after the dog is physically mature, which is generally around 12 - 15 months of age.

Step #2 — Run-Bys

When the dog is jumping toward you readily on your first command, you are ready to progress to run-bys.

Start with your dog in a sit-stay or with your assistant holding the dog in position. Take the leash in your hand and lead out a foot or so from the other side of the jump. Face your body in the direction your dog will be jumping, while looking at your dog over your shoulder. Extend your arm horizontally as much as possible to provide some distance between you and the jump.

Making sure you have your dog's attention, give him your command to jump and start moving forward. If necessary, your assistant can launch a dog that needs some extra help. Praise and reward.

As your dog gains confidence, reduce the amount of your lead-out until you are starting even with your dog. Make sure your arm remains high and extended so that you can stay away from the jump as much as possible, and so that you will not accidentally knock down the jump side support.

When the dog is jumping without hesitation on your command with no guidance from your leash, replace the leash with a tab (you must have off-leash control to progress to this point). Use the hand closest to the dog to give a flat-hand signal for the jump. The signal should be steady and deliberate — not flashing, waving, or swinging. Make sure all parts of your body (shoulders and feet) are facing slightly inward.

Step #3 — Adding Angles and Distance

If your dog is jumping smoothly when set up in a straight approach to the jump, it is time to work on increasing jump angles and distances. Begin this stage before the dog has begun to jump full height. Distance training is best accomplished with your dog off-lead and wearing a tab; therefore, off-leash control is required.

CALLING

First begin by calling your dog to you over the jump at various angles. Begin with mild angles and progress to more difficult ones.

Gradually increase the distance between your dog and the obstacle until he is beginning from a point 30 feet from the jump. Then, gradually adjust your position so that the jump is not directly between you and the dog when calling. He must take a line to the jump from your signal, verbal command, and body language. This is referred to as an **offset start.** (Figure 8-2.) Be sure to use a signal and proper body language to cue the dog (facing between the dog's current position and the obstacle you want him to take).

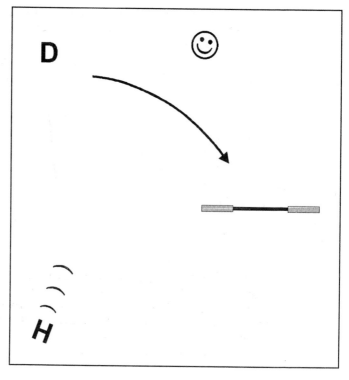

*Figure 8-2: Gradually adjust your position so that the jump is not directly between you and the dog when calling. This is referred to as an **offset start**. Remember to face the path your dog will be taking (indicated by the smiley face) rather than the obstacle when you give your command.*

SENDING

Once the dog is comfortable with you calling him over the jump at various angles and distances, you can begin to send him. As in the calling exercise, the jump height should remain low.

Show the dog a loaded target placed about 10 - 15 feet past the jump. Then position him about 10 - 15 feet in front of the jump.

Position yourself even with the dog but out to the side, facing the path you want him to take. Have an assistant hold your dog or place him in a sit-stay. If you have no assistant or reliable stay you can start with the dog at your side (sending *on the fly* as described in *Chapter 5* for the open tunnel).

Give your command to jump and begin moving forward. When the dog is in mid-air over the jump, release him to the target with *Get it!* Instead of running all the way to the target with the dog, hang back. Do not come to an abrupt stop. Instead, come to a gliding halt with one foot in front of the other. With each successful repetition you should be able to hang back more and more until you are able to remain in your approximate starting position while the dog completes the jump.

> **TRAINING TIP:** *Don't try this without a target in the learning stages. You may inadvertently teach your dog to curl back to you after being sent to an obstacle. If this behavior becomes habitual it can result in check-backs, refusals, knocked bars, and an inefficient jumping style.*

IF YOU HAVE PROBLEMS...

...If at any time the dog does not take the jump on your first command, don't repeat it. Give your unemotional verbal correction, then calmly take the dog's tab and return to your starting position. Focus his attention on the jump, give your jump command with enthusiasm and immediately launch toward the jump with a quick pop and release. Give immediate praise for taking the jump!

On your next attempt, do something to make the dog more likely to be successful, such as:

- Lower the jump height.

- Place the target closer to the jump or show the dog a larger or more enticing target.

- Do a restrained recall (have your assistant restrain the dog while exciting the dog with *Ready?*).

- Do a restrained send-away (restrain the dog while focusing his attention on an enticing target using an excited tone of voice).

Remember to always quit on a successful note.

PARALLEL DISTANCE

Work toward teaching the dog to perform the jump with you at gradually increasing parallel distances. Your dog will be taking a line from your signal and body position. Be careful to use proper body language. You do not want to couple incorrect cues with the behavior you want the dog to perform.

Step #4 — Spread Jumps

Spread jumps include a double-bar jump and a triple-bar jump. To successfully perform the obstacle, the dog must jump two or more bars spread a given distance apart. It's best to introduce the dog to spread jumps only after he is comfortable clearing single jumps.

Some spreads may be parallel, while others may be ascending. The parallel spreads are often more challenging than the ascending spreads, since the depth of the jump is not as readily apparent to the dog.

Start narrow and gradually add to the width of the spread. You can construct your spread jumps from single jumps placed close to one another. This will give you the flexibility to gradually add to the width of the spread as your dog gains confidence. Begin with recalls, then progress to run-bys. Eventually increase the jump angles and distance as described above.

Step #5 — Adding Height

When your dog is doing reliable recalls, run-bys, and send-aways on a tab at a variety of angles and distances, you are ready to start increasing the height of the jump. Don't be in a hurry to raise the jump height. Your dog will be a smarter, more reliable, and confident jumper if you give him plenty of experience jumping at low and very gradually increasing heights.

For small dogs, it's best to raise the jump only one inch at a time. For larger, fully grown dogs, you can increase the height in two-inch increments until the dog is within six inches of his full height. Then increase the height only one inch at a time.

Each time you raise the jump height, start with recalls and then progress to run-bys. Remain at that jump height for a minimum of a week. When the dog can perform recalls and run-bys off either side without launching assistance and without hesitation, you are ready to progress to the next higher height.

When raising the jump height, the gap between the ground and the jump bar will increase. Some dogs may be tempted to run under the bar instead of jumping it. To prevent this from happening, fill in the gap with bars at lower heights. When your dog has become comfortable at his full jump height, you can start to remove the lower bars one by one. He will eventually be required to jump his full height without any fill-in bars below.

> **TRAINING TIP:** *If your dog decides that he prefers traveling under the top bar as the lower bars are removed, drape clear plastic sheeting over the bar or position wire guides on the ground as a barrier. He will soon decide that it is much more fun to jump over the bar than to run under it.*

MONITORING THE DOG'S JUMPING STYLE

While working toward full-height jumping, keep an eye on the dog's jumping style. There is no one correct jumping style for all dogs; the way a dog jumps will depend in many ways on his size, shape, and structure. To be a smart jumper, the dog's take-off point is important. When dogs take off too early they are said to be **jumping flat.** When they take off too late they are they are said to be **popping** or **flat-footing** the jump. Either situation can cause problems in agility.

• Jumping flat can cause a dog to knock bars and can make him land so far past the jump that it is difficult to make a tight turn to the next obstacle.

• Popping jumps slows the dog down tremendously. It also places enormous stress on the dog's joints as he takes off and lands. You can often hear dogs that pop jumps make a grunting sound as they land. Your dog is most likely popping jumps if his take-off point is closer to the jump than the overall height of the jump.

The ideal jumper neither pops jumps nor takes off too early as a matter of habit. Experienced dogs learn to adjust their take-off point to the conditions of the course. When spacing is generous, the ideal take-off should be flatter. Too flat, however, and knocked bars may occur.

When spacing is tight or sharp turns are required, the smart jumper will perform a more rounded jump. A perfectly rounded jump is one in which the dog takes off and lands at a point that is approximately the same distance to the jump as the height of the jump. Flattening slightly from a rounded jump, however, may be preferable on the agility course for the majority of situations, since it will lessen the impact on the dog's joints and help increase speed.

> **TRAINING TIP:** *Many agility jumps contain bar supports at four- or six-inch intervals rather than one- or two-inch intervals. Do not be tempted to increase your dog's jump height in four- or six-inch increments out of convenience! You may adversely affect your dog's jumping style. It is quite common to see such dogs take off too close to the jump because they have not been allowed to gradually become accustomed to taking off from a greater distance from the jump. They also may tend to jump higher than necessary, which slows the dog down.*

You can increase the height of the bar in small increments using an inexpensive jump fashioned from two stick-in-the-ground weave poles, using large binder clips for bar supports.

ADJUSTING THE DOG'S TAKE-OFF POINT

Some dogs are naturally great jumpers from the start. Most others learn to jump well through experimentation and practice. Typically, what feels best to the dog is his best jumping style. A few dogs, however, need help from their handlers in finding that ideal style. For dogs that habitually take off too early or too late, ground bars may be helpful.

For a dog that takes off too close to the jump, place a jump bar on the ground at the place where he has been taking off (Figure 8-3). This should force the dog to take off earlier. You can experiment to find the ideal position for the ground bar on successive attempts by moving it slightly toward or away from the jump until you find the right setup for your dog. Measure the distance from the bar to the jump. From this point, place ground bars at this distance on the approach side of every jump until the dog becomes accustomed to his new and improved take-off point.

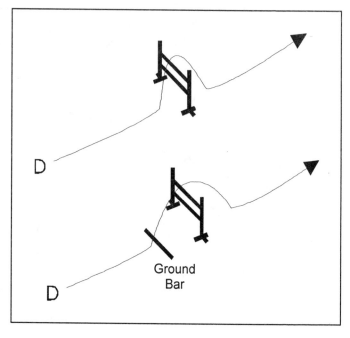

Figure 8-3: For dogs that "pop" jumps. A ground bar encourages an earlier take-off.

For dogs that take off too early, position the ground bar so that the dog must take a step over the bar before leaving the ground to jump (Figure 8-4). Experiment to find the optimum distance until the dog can no longer jump over both the ground bar and the jump. For some dogs, this will be quite a distance from the obstacle. When the dog is stepping over the ground bar and then jumping, you can gradually move the bar slightly closer to the jump until his take-off point is most ideal. Measure this distance and place ground bars on the approach side of every jump until the dog becomes accustomed to his new style of jumping.

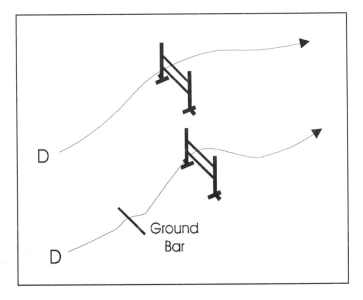

Figure 8-4: A ground bar can help a "flat" jumper to perform a more rounded jump.

Understand that these are not quick fixes — especially if you have not been vigilant and have allowed your dog to jump incorrectly over a long period of time. It may take weeks or months for your dog to develop the muscle memory to form a habit of jumping more efficiently. You cannot expect results overnight.

OTHER FIXES FOR JUMPING PROBLEMS

Sometimes a dog may display a tendency to knock bars, even though his take-offs and degree of roundness/flatness while jumping seem appropriate for the situation. In these cases, the dog may be skimming the top of the jump with his front or back feet. He may not be aware that it is important to you that he keep his feet tucked until he has completely cleared the bar.

Some incentives to help your dog pick up his feet include:

- Construct some heavy jump bars by filling PVC pipe with sand and sealing them with end-caps. If the dog displaces the bar he will feel a correction against his feet.

- Use invisible monofilament (fishing line) "jump heighteners" positioned about ½" - 1" above the bar. For your dog's safety, attach the monofilament to the wings or jump side supports using sewing elastic, so that the line will give way if the dog snags it with his foot.

Monofilament "jump heightener."

- Place wire guides over the top bar, tent-style. The wire will extend above the bar, effectively raising the height of the jump by ¾" to 1". The dog must clear the bar by this margin or he will feel the wire rub against his feet.

- Hold onto the bar as the dog is jumping and raise it slightly upward to touch the offending feet as he clears it. (This method works best if you have an assistant raise the other side of the bar at the same time.)

- Act shocked and surprised that your dog has actually knocked a bar! Stop and give him an immediate opportunity to clear it successfully.

- Pick up the bar and scold it. Believe it or not, many dogs will work harder the next time to keep the bar from getting in trouble again!

Wire guides placed over jump bar.

When faced with a bar-knocking problem, it is crucial that you do not ignore displaced bars. Each and every time a bar falls, stop immediately and address it. If you ignore the displaced bar because you are trying to work on another skill or concept, you have reinforced the dog for knocking it. As such you have thwarted your goal of communicating to your dog that clearing bars is important.

When working on another skill or on handling, it is a good idea to keep the bars set at a low height so that it will be less likely that your dog will displace a bar.

Step #6 — Disguising the Jumps

In your many travels to agility trials you will undoubtedly encounter jumps decorated in the most elaborate ways imaginable. Some jumps include wings decorated with realistic giant cats, howling wolves, leaping dogs, rainbows, and silk flowers. Other jumps are decorated to commemorate events or holidays. As an added challenge, some jumps include garlands or streamers or other elements that move with the wind. If your dog has not been trained to confidently soar over anything and everything vaguely resembling a jump, you cannot consider him fully trained. When you travel to an agility trial across the country, you don't want to have to cross your fingers and hope that the jumps you will encounter are plain and conventional. The answer? Decorate your own jumps in training and work through any problems.

Use your imagination to transform your familiar training jumps into strange and elaborate ones. Drape clothing or linens around the wings. Add scarves, pinwheels or crepe paper that will move or make noise with the wind. Place potted plants, silk flowers, or children's punching bags in front of the wings. Anything that is safe and that does not obstruct the dog's ability to jump is fair game.

During your dress-up-the-jump sessions, don't forget to have someone kneel down beside the wing and hold up a bar for the dog to jump. This is a scenario that is likely to occur should your dog knock down a bar and then re-attempt the jump before the steward has a chance to completely replace it.

Broad (Long) Jump

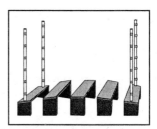

General Rules

The dog must enter be-
tween the first two upright
marker poles and exit between the second two marker poles.
Stepping on or displacing any of the broad jump boards is
faulted. Entering or exiting incorrectly is scored as a refusal.

There are two styles of broad jumps. In the **hogback** style,
pictured above, the highest board is in located in the center of
the jump, with the height of the adjacent boards gradually de-
creasing. The **ascending** style, pictured on the following
pages, contains boards that gradually increase in height, end-
ing with the highest board. Since each of these jumps presents
a different sight picture to the dog, it is important to train with
both types of jumps.

Commands

For simplicity's sake, many people use the same command for
the broad jump as they use for all the other jumps. Others
choose a separate command for the broad jump because it
has a distinct sight picture and the dogs can distinguish it from
the other jumps. Either philosophy can be successful, so
choose a command that feels right to you.

Setting Up the Broad Jump

For all of your initial training, set the broad jump at a very
short length. A length that is roughly equivalent to the height
of the jumps your dog is currently jumping is a good place to
start.

Position a wingless bar jump with a low-set bar about mid-
way over the broad jump. This will help the dog realize that
the broad jump is actually a jump and not a contact obstacle.

It will also encourage the dog to jump with an arc centered on the jump bar. Eventually you will progress to placing the bar directly on the broad jump board, then removing the bar completely.

To begin your broad jump training, position a wingless bar jump with a low-set bar mid-way over the jump.

In some styles of agility, dogs are faulted if they tick the last board of the broad jump. A good way to help prevent this from becoming a problem for your dog is to position a jump-extending aid beyond the last board for your initial training as well as all subsequent training.

The following photos show the positioning of jump-extending aids. Wire guides can be placed under the last board such that they protrude several inches beyond the board. Alternatively, several scrub brushes or one long push-broom brush can be placed at the last board in a similar fashion. With either of these devices, if the dog does not clear the board by a generous margin, the dog's feet will make contact with the wire or brush. Many dogs will find the sensation unpleasant, although the effect is harmless to the dog.

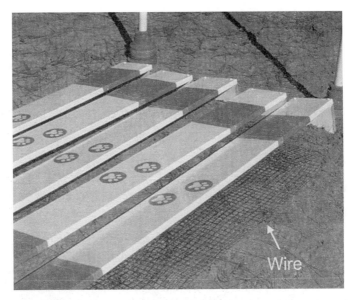

Position flattened wire guides under the last broad jump board to condition the dog to completely clear it.

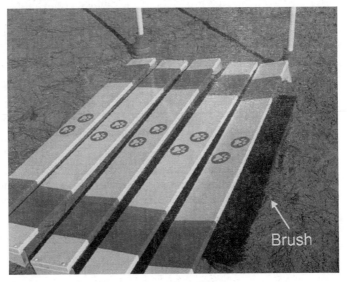

A large push broom brush or a set of smaller scrub brushes can also pattern the dog to clear the broad jump.

It is best if the aids are positioned such that the dog cannot see them until after he has taken off for the jump. This way, the sight picture in training will be identical to the one the dog will encounter in competition.

Steps #1 and #2 — Recalls and Run-Bys

Follow the procedures described for recalls and run-bys over jumps.

Steps #3 and 4 — Adding Angles and Distance and Increasing Width

Follow the steps described for jumps for adding angles and distance, using a short-length broad jump. Once the dog is doing well, begin to add to the length of the jump very gradually. For each new length, start with recalls, followed by run-bys, then angles and distance. Work on calling, sending, and parallel distance.

Eventually, the broad jump will be long enough for your dog to enter or exit incorrectly through the marker poles, especially on an angled approach. Use wire guides or other barriers to pattern a straight approach and to keep your dog jumping in a straight line through the broad jump. (Figure 8-5.) As always, when you give your command and signal, remember to face the path (indicated by the smiley face) rather than the obstacle.

IF YOUR DOG EXPERIENCES PROBLEMS

If the dog walks over the broad jump boards rather than jumping them, don't let him repeat the mistake. Instead, try one of the following:

- Make the jump length shorter so that it is easier for the dog to succeed.

- Do a restrained recall or a restrained send-away to a target to increase the dog's impulsion.

- Place flattened wire guides or another unpleasant but safe material on top of the broad jump boards.

- Turn one or more of the broad jump boards on their sides so that it will not be possible to walk over them.

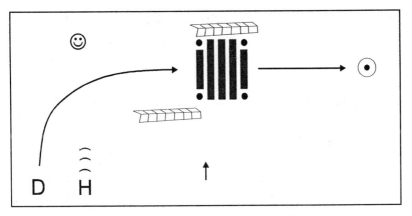

Figure 8-5: Sending over the broad jump at an angle to a target.

Tire Jump

PICTURE OF PERFECT PERFORMANCE

The dog soars cleanly through the tire opening without hesitation and from a variety of angles.

General Rules

The dog must jump through the tire in the direction indicated by the judge. Jumping between the tire and the frame in the correct direction is scored as a refusal. Doing the same in the incorrect direction is faulted as a wrong course. No fault is incurred for the dog touching or banking off the bottom of the tire.

Commands

The tire jump is different from the other jumps in that the dog must jump through a precise opening, rather than over the top of a bar or board. It also has a unique appearance from the other obstacles on the course. Because your dog can easily recognize the unique shape of the tire jump, it should have its own unique command.

Common commands are *Tire!* and *Through!* Do not use *Through!* if it is the command you use for one of the tunnels. These obstacles are clearly distinguishable from one another and should have separate commands.

Step #1 — Recalls

Set the tire at a very low height. It should be just high enough for the dog to hop through. With your dog on lead, have an assistant hold him directly in front of the tire opening and thread your leash through to the opposite side.

Go to the other side of the tire opening, take the leash and establish friendly eye contact with your dog through the tire. Give your command while tapping the bottom of the inside rim of the tire and then backing up. Your assistant can help launch the dog if necessary. Praise and reward.

For a dog that is reluctant, it can help to use an incentive. Shake a plastic food container or squeak a toy through the tire opening. When he hops through, reward him by tossing it a short distance.

Training the tire jump.

Step #2 — Run-Bys

With your dog on leash at your left side, start about ten feet from the entry to the tire. Your path toward the obstacle will be important. As a handler, you want to avoid taking a path that runs you into the tire frame. If you do, you will either stop abruptly, which may cause your dog to stop as well, or you will start to turn away from the obstacle as you approach to avoid getting trapped. When you turn away, your dog is very likely to do the same. To prevent this from happening, start slightly to the right of the obstacle so that your path will be angling slightly inward toward the tire. Your path should allow you to continue past the tire smoothly without getting trapped behind it or turning away (Figure 8-7).

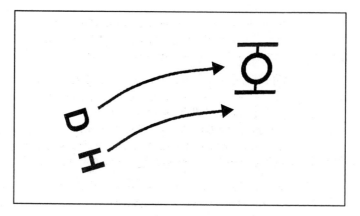

Figure 8-7: When training run-bys on the tire jump, take a path that makes it easy for the dog to succeed.

Hold your dog's leash close to the collar and focus his attention ahead to the tire. Give your command and start moving toward the obstacle. You will be "bowling" your dog through the tire opening. As the dog commits, let go of the leash and continue moving past the tire. Meet him on the other side with plenty of praise and a reward.

If your dog has trouble — for example, if he wants to jump between the tire and the frame or if he is reluctant to jump at all — have your assistant use an incentive as described for recalls.

> **TRAINING TIP:** *When performing run-bys with the tire jump, do not throw the toy through the tire opening! You could easily miss the opening and send it ricocheting back to you. Worse yet, your dog could injure himself or his confidence by ramming his head into the tire as he focuses on the thrown object.*

Step #3 — Increasing the Height

The tire requires a precision jump from the dog — the jump he makes must be neither too high nor too low. Don't be in a hurry to raise the tire height too quickly. Doing so can cause confidence problems and can result in dogs who prefer to run underneath the tire rather than through it.

When your dog can do run-bys at a given height off both sides and without any "bowling" from you, you are ready to start raising the tire height. For small dogs, this means no more than one inch at a time. Larger dogs can progress in two-inch increments until they approach their full height. For the last six inches you should progress only one inch at a time.

At some point as you train the tire, almost every dog will realize that it is possible to go under the tire or between the tire and the frame. This is to be expected. If and when this happens, prevent the dog from repeating his mistake by blocking the opening with wire guides or other material.

As with the all the other obstacles, be sure to work equally off the right as you do off the left.

Steps #4 & 5 — Adding Angles and Distance

As you have trained with the other obstacles, progress until you can call and send your dog to perform the tire jump from a distance of 30 feet, at a variety of angles.

When the obstacles are mastered, the real fun begins!

_9_ Where to Go From Here

Congratulations! You have taken the first important step toward excelling in the agility ring! By now, you and your canine companion have developed a solid foundation in obstacle training. The care you have taken to provide a thoughtful and systematic foundation will repay you many times over in the months and years ahead. What's more, you have developed a happy working relationship with your dog based on trust, consistency, mutual respect, and high expectations.

If any of the concepts presented in this book have been less than perfectly clear to you, it may help to view the appropriate sections in the corresponding video, _Competitive Agility with Jane Simmons-Moake — Tape 1: Obstacle Training_. To help you locate specific topics, a _Video Topic Guide_ is provided in Appendix B.

Once you have mastered all of the skills _in Book 1: Obstacle Training_, you are ready to progress to _Excelling at Dog Agility — Book 2: Sequence Training_.

Puppy testing can help you predict a dog's potential as a future working partner.

Appendix A: Volhard Puppy Aptitude Test

On the following pages you will find a copy of the Volhard *Puppy Aptitude Test,* reprinted with permission from its creator, Wendy Volhard. This system helps determine a puppy's basic temperament traits while helping to predict his potential as a future working partner.

Interpreting the Scores for Agility

Each puppy receives a score of 1 to 6 for each of eleven sub-tests. There are no ideal scores that apply to every trainer and every working situation. There are, however, some generalizations that can be made with respect to a puppy's suitability as a competitive agility dog.

- Dogs scoring mostly 6's are independent and may be very difficult and frustrating to train.

- Dogs scoring mostly 5's are also not well-suited to agility training. They may be overly submissive, easily stressed, and concerned about their environment.

- Dogs scoring mostly 4's will most likely be easy to train, however, lack the competitive potential of the more active, outgoing dogs scoring 3's or higher. These dogs may be good choices for first-time dog trainers or children, or for those who prefer a more sedate dog with which to live.

- Dogs scoring mostly 3's are the best prospect for the average owner. They are outgoing and active, accept humans as leaders easily, adapt well to new situations, and will most likely be responsive and fun to train.

- Dogs scoring mostly 3's with a few 2's may be a very good choice for an experienced trainer who is looking for competitive scores. These dogs have the trainability and willingness of the 3's, with some added spark and stamina for a competitive edge. This is the type of dog that is often chosen for police work or drug-detection. They may be slightly "too much dog" however, for a first-time trainer.

- Dogs scoring mostly 2's often have bouncy, outgoing temperaments and will easily withstand the rigors of intensive training, However, they can be dominant and require firm, consistent handling and an experienced trainer.

- Dog's scoring mostly 1's can be highly dominant and may have aggressive tendencies. They may be very difficult to train and require a very experienced, firm, consistent handler.

- For the *Energy Level* Test, choose a puppy with at least a medium energy level if your goal is competitive agility. A puppy that scores high on energy level will be your best competitive choice if your goal is to excel in the agility ring.

For more detailed information about conducting and evaluating results from the Puppy Aptitude Test, refer to The Idiot's Guide to Dog Training *by Jack and Wendy Volhard, Macmillan Publishing, 1999.*

You can also refer to the booklet entitled Puppy Selection, *available from the Volhard's Top Dog Training School, 30 Besaw Road, Phoenix, NY, 13135.*

Volhard Puppy Aptitude Test

TEST	PURPOSE	SCORE	
SOCIAL ATTRACTION: Place the puppy in a test area. From a few feet away the tester coaxes the pup to her/him by clapping hands gently and kneeling down. Tester must coax in a direction away from the point where it entered the testing area.	Degree of attraction to people, confidence, or dependence.	Came readily, tail up, jumped, bit at hands	1
		Came readily, tail up, pawed, licked at hands	2
		Came readily tail up	3
		Came readily, tail down	4
		Came hesitantly, tail down	5
		Didn't come at all	6
FOLLOWING: Stand up and walk away from the pup in a normal manner. Make sure the pup sees you walk away.	Degree of willingness to follow human leadership. Not following Indicates independence.	Followed readily, tail up, got underfoot, bit at feet	1
		Followed readily, tail up, got underfoot	2
		Followed readily, tail down	3
		Followed hesitantly, tail down	4
		No follow or went away	5
			6
RESTRAINT: Crouch down and gently roll the pup on his back and hold it with one hand for a full 30 seconds.	Degree of dominant or submissive tendency. How it accepts stress when socially/physically dominated.	Struggled fiercely, flailed, bit	1
		Struggled fiercely, flailed	2
		Settled, struggled, settled with some eye contact	3
		Struggled then settled	4
		No struggle	5
		No struggle, straining to avoid eye contact	6

TEST	PURPOSE	SCORE	
SOCIAL DOMINANCE: Let pup stand up and gently stroke him from the head to back while you crouch beside him. Continue stroking until a recognizable behavior is established.	Degree of acceptance of human social dominance. How "forgiving" the pup is.	Jumped, pawed, bit, growled	1
		Jumped, pawed	2
		Cuddles up to tester and tries to lick face	3
		Squirmed, licked at hands	4
		Rolled over, licked at hands	5
		Went away and stayed away	6
ELEVATION DOMINANCE: Bend over and cradle the pup under its belly, fingers interlaced, palms up and elevate it just off the ground. Hold it there for 30 seconds.	Degree of accepting dominance while in position of no control.	Struggled fiercely, bit, growled	1
		Struggled fiercely	2
		No struggle, relaxed	3
		Struggled, settled, licked	4
		No struggle, licked at hands	5
		No struggle, froze	6
RETRIEVING: Crouch beside the pup and attract his attention with crumpled up paper ball. When the pup shows interest and is watching, toss the object 4-6 feet in front of the pup.	Degree of willingness to work with a human. High correlation between ability to retrieve and successful guide dogs, obedience dogs, field trial dogs.	Chases object, picks up object and runs away	1
		Chases object, stands over object, does not return	2
		Chases object and returns with object to tester	3
		Chases object and returns without object to tester	4
		Starts to chase object, loses interest	5
		Does not chase object	6
TOUCH SENSITIVITY: Take the puppy's webbing of one front foot and press between finger and thumb lightly, then more firmly, until you get a response.	Degree of sensitivity to touch	8-10 counts before response	1
		6-7 counts before response	2
		5-6 counts before response	3
		2-4 counts before response	4
		1-2 counts before response	5

TEST	PURPOSE	SCORE	
SOUND SENSITIVITY: Place pup in center of area, tester or assistant makes a sharp noise a few feet from puppy. A large metal spoon struck sharply on a metal pan works well.	Degree of sensitivity to sound. (Also can be rudimentary test for deafness).	Listens, locates sound, walks toward it barking	1
		Listens, locates sound, barks	2
		Listens, locates sound, shows curiosity and walks toward sound	3
		Listens, locates the sound	4
		Cringes, backs off, hides	5
		Ignores sound, shows no curiosity	6
CHASE INSTINCT: Place pup in center of area. Tie a string around a large towel and jerk it across the floor a few feet away from puppy.	Degree of response to moving object; chase instinct.	Looks, attacks and bites	1
		Looks, barks and tail up	2
		Looks curiously, attempts to investigate	3
		Looks, barks, tail tucked	4
		Runs away, hides	5
		Ignores sound, shows no curiosity	6
STABILITY: Place pup in center of area. Closed umbrella is held 4 feet away and pointed perpendicular to the direction the pup faces. The umbrella is opened and set down so the pup can investigate.	Degree of intelligent response to strange object.	Walks forward, tail up, bites	1
		Walks forward, tail up, mouths	2
		Walks forward, attempts to investigate	3
		Looks curiously, stays put	4
		Goes away, tail down, hides	5
		Ignores, shows no curiosity	6
ENERGY LEVEL: Observe pup on the other subtests and score according to the most frequent activity observed. Check with breeder for confirmation.	Degree of physical energy	Continually runs, pounces, wiggles, paws	HIGH
		Mostly trots, occasionally runs, pounces, wiggles	MED
		Walks slowly, sits quietly, remains in position	LOW
		Stands rigidly, eyes roll, tail down, ears back	STRESS

Appendix B: Video Topic Guide – Tape 1

Below is a listing of topics from the companion video to this book, *Competitive Agility with Jane Simmons-Moake, Tape 1: Obstacle Training*. For each topic there is a corresponding number listed to help you quickly find the section of your choice. The number refers to the counter on most video playback units, indicating the time elapsed (hour:minute:second). To use the video topic guide, rewind the tape and press *counter reset* to set the counter to zero. Then fast-forward to the time indicated on the chart.

Topic	Time
Crunchy agility	4:47
Smooth agility	5:47
Unwanted behaviors	6:34
Training with a partner	7:47
Tone of voice	8:08
Using rewards	8:26
Training tools	9:10
Collars	9:15
Tabs	9:38
Treats & toys	9:43
Targets	10:17
Food containers	10:30
Wire guides & hoops	10:38

Obstacle training principles	11:10
Open tunnel	13:50
Closed tunnel	22:14
Pause table	24:25
Weave poles	31:23
Contact obstacles	44:40
A-Frame	49:28
Dog walk	56:45
See-saw	59:50
Jumps	1:03:12
Ground bars	1:08:49
Heavy bars, monofilament	1:10:19
Dressing up jumps	1:11:00
Broad jump	1:11:17
Tire jump	1:13:30
Agility fun-fest and credits	1:16:30

What the agility world is saying about the award-winning video series:

Competitive Agility Training
with
Jane Simmons-Moake

"Finally I have found a series of tapes that not only shows every step of the way in getting to the desired goal but demonstrates these steps over and over, until you thoroughly understand how to get there and also the pitfalls to avoid. I can unabashedly recommend the Jane Simmons-Moake Competitive Agility Training tapes to all who have ever considered taking up agility, are currently doing agility or merely want to learn more about it."

"...I have frequently purchased videos that I watched once and then put aside. Not this time! ... I will refer frequently to the beautifully detailed instruction in these tapes."

"...Sequences of actual trials are also included and really helped me to put into reality why particular sequences were so essential to teach."

"...Not only is the content superb, the quality of the tapes is excellent and the filming locale varied... they are a delight to watch."

Helen Phillips, *Front and Finish* and *Borderlines*

"The videos are so packed with info it would take you a year to do all the exercises and perfect your handling. I think people are insane not to own these videos."

"...THEY ARE SOOO AWESOME. I would highly recommend them to any agility enthusiast."

Angelica E. Steinker, M. Ed.

"Even if you never, ever in your lifetime intend to do competitive Agility training, I still DEMAND that you own this video [Tape 1] if you want to...

♦ Get inside the head of any dog.
♦ Have a dog understand and eagerly respond to your commands.
♦ Have a faster, happier working Obedience dog.
♦ Have a faster, more responsive Schutzund dog.
♦ Have a happier pet and companion."

"...Ms. Moake has written a script loaded with simple, easy-to-understand rationale for both dog and handler."

"...This video shows example after example of excellent trainers and top-working dogs and explains how they get to the high stature in the Agility community. Better yet, it anticipates and shows by several examples the many common mistakes made so that you can nip those mistakes in the bud — before you make them."

Robin Stark, Rottweiler Quarterly

"...Without doubt the most comprehensive how-to agility video project on the U.S. market to date..."

Elise Paffrath, Clean Run Magazine

"If you want to start getting involved in agility training with your dog or you already are but could use some expert instruction, you cannot do better than to learn from Jane Simmons-Moake, one of the best and most successful agility handlers."

"...This is one of those exceptional productions in which everything is well-done."

"...I would recommend this set of tapes for everyone's agility library."

Gayle George-Sackett, AKC Gazette

Competitive Agility Training with Jane Simmons-Moake

This award-winning video series:

- Provides step-by-step instruction from beginning to ultra-advanced agility training.

- Professionally produced by Canine Training Systems, these are tapes you will want to watch again and again.

- Features training demonstrations using 26 breeds, 70 dogs, and 43 handlers.

- Includes both positive and negative examples to illustrate the consequences of handling choices.

Jane's methods:

- Focus on smooth excellence from the start.

- Emphasize skill-building to isolate and train essential dog and handler skills.

- Place early emphasis on distance handling to take advantage of the dog's speed.

- Result in competitive success for people of all ages, shapes, and sizes.

- Are motivational and fun!

Jane Simmons-Moake is one of the world's foremost agility trainers. A top-winning competitor, veteran judge, and award-winning author, Jane runs one of the nation's most successful agility training organizations, FlashPaws Agility Training Center in Houston, Texas. A popular seminar leader in the U.S. and abroad, Jane has also competed internationally as a member of the 1996 and 1997 U.S World Championship Agility Teams.

COMPETITIVE AGILITY TRAINING

with

Jane Simmons-Moake

Bill Newcomb

Named "Best Video Production of 1998" by the Dog Writers' Association of America

Tape 1: Obstacle Training

Teach your dog to master each obstacle with competitive excellence in mind. Includes important principles for building a strong foundation for all of your agility training. (80 mins.)

Tape 2: Sequence Training

Discover how to sequence smoothly from one obstacle to the next, to reach your dog's highest potential for speed and accuracy. (78 mins.)

Tape 3: Advanced Skills Training

Learn how to isolate and train many of the skills necessary to compete at the highest levels. (80 mins.)

Each tape is $59.95 (+ $4.50 U.S. Priority Mail shipping and handling for up to 3 tapes)
OR save $30 when you order all three! TX orders add 7-1/4% tax.

_____Tape 1: Obstacle Training
_____Tape 2: Sequence Training
_____Tape 3: Advanced Skills Training

Name _____

Address _____

City _____

State_____   Zip _____

Telephone/Fax _____

Mail check or money order (U.S. funds only) to: FlashPaws,
7714 Rolling Fork Lane, Houston, TX 77040-3432
Visa and MasterCard also accepted

Card #_____   Expiration _____

Name on card _____

(713) 896-8484 phone/fax, E-mail: JaneSM@aol.com
web site: www.flashpaws.com

For information about seminars, books, videos, and our complete line of supplies for the performance dog:

visit our web site at:
www.flashpaws.com

or contact:

FLASHPAWS

7714 Rolling Fork Lane .
Houston, TX 77040-3432
(713) 896-8484

E-mail: JaneSM@aol.com